Tainted Legacy

The Story of Alleged Serial Killer Bertha Gifford

S. Kay Murphy

PublishAmerica
Baltimore

First printing

PublishAmerica has allowed this work to remain exactly as the author intended, verbatim, without editorial input.

Hardcover 978-1-4489-8960-7
Softcover 1-60563-803-X
PUBLISHED BY PUBLISHAMERICA, LLLP
www.publishamerica.com
Baltimore

Printed in the United States of America

~ Mom ~

Here, at long last, is the story. In the end, there are many things to be regretted…but nothing to be ashamed of.

~ Shali, Joanna, Ezra and Sam ~

In you, my legacy is redeemed.

Acknowledgments

Words cannot adequately express my deepest thanks to the following:

To Mrs. Walton, my fourth grade teacher—and to all those teachers who are willing to encourage the gifts they see in their students: Please know that your contribution to our lives is enormous, and we never forget you, even if we never come back to thank you.

To Thomas Dawson, the author, as far as I have been able to discover, of the St. Louis Post-Dispatch articles on Bertha Gifford: Thank you for your exceptionally fine writing, your attention to detail, and your continuity. The story would be lost without your work.

To the unsung heroes who sit in, I'm sure, dimly lit rooms, copying page after page after page of old newspapers onto microfilm, and to those who tediously index each and every story: Writers and researchers will applaud you for generations to come.

To every librarian who smiled at my requests and didn't act too busy to help (though often you were): Thank you.

To Chris and Amanda, night clerks at the Holiday Inn Express in Pacific, Missouri: Thank you for watching out for me so my son wouldn't worry, and thanks especially for your kindness and enthusiasm.

To Bob, Rosella and Tim Fiedler: Thank you for all your gifts of time and resources and where they led me, and especially for your graciousness. I am honored to know you at long last.

To my new cousins, Jean Thompson and LaVerne Brinley Sheppard: Thank you for your love and affection and acceptance. If we don't meet here, I'll meet you over there.

To my old cousin Danny: You loved me. You believed in me. That's all I needed.

To Marc Houseman, who joins me in honoring the dead, and without whom portions of this book could not have been composed accurately. Thank you for reading my words…and for listening.

To my family of writers: Lola De Julio De Maci, Laura Slattery, Robert Louis Covington, Kathleen Shaputis, Bob Hasse, Libby Grandy, and Willma Gore. You have been sisters and brothers, fathers and mothers, sons and daughters to me for over a decade. Were it not for you all, I'm certain I would not have chosen to stay. I love you immensely. Thanks for always, always loving me in return. Special thanks to LJ for reading the first draft and leaving me a message that revived me every time I thought of giving up.

To my squad of cheerleaders: Michael Welker, Doug DeYoung, Denise Murphy, and Peggy Jackson—y'all have no idea how powerful your love has been for me.

And to the grandmothers who have guided me on this journey: I promise you that the legacy, from this generation forward, will be one of redemption.

Preface

If the newspaper reports, magazine articles, online postings and comic book features are true, my great-grandmother, Bertha Gifford, qualifies as America's first female serial killer. It is not my intention within these pages to sensationalize her crimes; the media has already done a thorough job of that, often forgetting or ignoring the many individuals and families that were torn apart by the actions of this outwardly benign grandmother from rural Missouri. But I think there is a compelling story here that has yet to be told in its entirety, and what makes it further compelling is the discovery of it from my perspective.

Imagine you'd been told that you are the direct descendant of a serial killer. Would it change the way you think about yourself or your family? Would you question what you might be capable of? Or at the very least, if any latent genetic predisposition to homicide languished in your DNA?

When I discovered that I had a grandparent who had spent the last years of her life in an institution for the criminally insane, I was compelled—no, driven would be more accurate—to discover why, for several reasons. First, because I love a good mystery, and her guilt had never been fully established—at least not to my mother's satisfaction. Second, because of an admitted romantic notion that I just might clear her name, if that were warranted. And last (though I only realized this after I began to write the book) because I needed to know more about my history so that I could understand more about myself.

This is a complex and convoluted story, with twists, turns and irony that is so bizarre at times it seems contrived or surreal. But it is just the sort of story I believe in, because it involves human experience in all of its range, including what is the best about us, and what is the worst about us. Beyond all the wonder about what was going through the mind of Bertha Gifford, there is a story here about people, average people living in rural America and struggling to balance the goodness and heartache of life as best they could with the resources they had. In order to fully understand, we have to remember that these events transpired during a much simpler time…a time when individuals depended on each other much more than we do today, and so were far less isolated than we might assume.

Prologue

For long moments there is no other sound in the car but the swishing metronome of the wipers across the windshield. The rain is steady, but light. Cornfields stretch out on either side of the road, though the terrain is not flat. Off to the east I can see cottonwoods growing along the riverbed.

We'd found the narrow bridge easily, just as the clerk in the small convenience store had described it. And when we'd pulled up to it and stopped, Mom had perked up, the light of recognition shining in her eyes for the first time in days.

"I remember this bridge," she said, hope in her voice. She hadn't been here in many years. At her comment, I'd glanced across to the passenger side of the small rental car and wondered if, had I reached the age of seventy-six, I would remember events that had happened when I was ten years old. It's true that we remember events quite vividly and for many years if they are catalyzed by intense emotion. My intuition suggests that my mother must have suffered great anguish and loss over the events that had begun on an August day so long ago.

Having negotiated the single-lane bridge, we travel slowly down the curving country road, looking for the farmhouse where my great-grandmother had lived with her second husband, Gene Gifford.

"Anything look familiar?" I ask, after we have gone some distance past the bridge in silence.

"I'm not sure," she replies hesitantly. "It all looks the same…I mean, it's all just typical farm country." She pauses, then sighs, irritated. "I don't know, the house is a hundred years old. I don't know if it would even still be there after all these years." Her eyes become distant, less hopeful again.

My mother, Ernestine, was a young girl when she lived in this rural community with her grandparents, Bertha and Gene Gifford and their son, James. Just four years older than my mother, Jim was more like a big brother than an uncle to her. Life on the farm where she could read, fish, and ride her black mare to her heart's content must have been idyllic. Chances are she would have grown up there—had her grandmother not been arrested for murder.

On a humid August day in 1928, an unfamiliar car pulled into the dirt driveway of the farmhouse and a solemn-faced man emerged. Jim and Ernestine, their game in the yard interrupted, followed him to the door as he knocked and was permitted to enter the house. My mother, who was ten at the time, trailed her grandmother into a bedroom and watched as she quietly powdered her face, then left the house with the man. Her grandmother and this stranger climbed into the car which moved off down the gravel road, the sound of the engine slowly receding in the quiet morning air.

Now, on an August day in 1994, we drive down a country road, my mother and I, searching for more than a house that may have been lost to time. My mother is searching for answers to questions she has had for decades. I have come first in search of the story which has never been told. And I am equally driven by the need to discover anything which might help me understand more fully my ancestry, the chemistry and biology from which I have been derived. More specifically, I need to know if this family history and genetic legacy defines who I am—or will be.

Questions hover between us now as we look for the house which is both crime scene and beloved childhood home. A sense of gloom envelops me as I peer through the rain on the windshield and begin to feel immured by the dark clouds and severely isolated countryside.

"This looks familiar!" my mother's unexpected exclamation jars me from my thoughts.

"What part?" I ask. The scene seems unchanged.

"I don't know…all of it…." Her voice trails off. Then, "If this is where I think it is, we'll go around a bend, and the house will be there." All my senses are alerted.

"It's a white farmhouse with a red barn," she says, reiterating the same description she has given me several times in the course of our drive. I again resist the urge to remind her that we are driving through rural Missouri. There are thousands of white farmhouses and hundreds of red barns.

Then, as if she's seen it in a vision, we roll around a curve in the road, and there it is: a stately white farmhouse appearing nearly gothic as we view it through the huge trees which closely guard it. A hundred feet away stands a large red barn.

Chapter One
"Like Our Great-Grandmother"

It is an odd thing to have a family member who is a murderer, even more odd that the family member was a simple farm woman—a grandmother. When I reveal to people that my great-grandmother would have been considered, in today's terms, a serial killer, they look at me just a little differently. But I never hesitate to be forthcoming with the truth—now that I know it. For my mother, who spent significant years of her childhood being raised by Bertha Gifford, it was a different story. When her grandmother was taken to jail, my mother knew instinctively, as children often know these things, that she was not to talk about it. She maintained her silence for decades, rarely speaking of that part of her life, even after she married and had children of her own. As a child, and even more so as an adult, I wondered on occasion why my mother rarely spoke of her own childhood and why she always seemed reluctant to discuss her side of the family in the same way my proud Irish father discussed his.

Then one day when I was thirty-five I was sitting at my dining room table, engaged in a casual conversation with my sister over a glass of iced tea. I don't remember now what it was I said that prompted her remark. It was some comment made in jest about my questionable sanity.

"Like our great-grandmother," was my sister's flippant response.

"We had a great-grandmother who was insane?" I asked, not taking her seriously.

"Well, yes," she replied, "the one who killed all those people."

13

I've never forgotten the conversation or that moment. The seconds ticked away after her last statement, each of us reading the other's face. I can still see her eyes as she realized that this was new information for me. At some point in time, my mother had told her at least a fragment of the story of Bertha Gifford. She had never mentioned it to me.

Of course I asked my mother about it the next time I spoke with her. As I expected, she was reluctant to give details, and glossed over it quickly, telling me her grandmother had been accused of poisoning some people, but they were "down and outers" from the community, and she thought the murders had been mercy killings.

We didn't discuss it again for several years. I was a single parent raising four teenaged children, teaching school, working on a graduate degree, and trying to recover from an unexpected divorce. My days were filled with the stress of working, parenting and being a student. I thought little about the fact that some old woman who was a distant relative had been accused of murder, especially since her alleged crimes had taken place during an era in which forensic science was far less precise than it is today.

Then, on a mid-winter night in 1993, my sister-in-law called to let me know that my mother had been hospitalized with pneumonia. I drove out to see her the next day.

She was sleeping when I got there, so I sat quietly next to her bed. She looked weak and pale, but when she woke up and saw me, she smiled. We had been talking for awhile about how she was feeling when she surprised me by bringing up the subject of her grandmother.

"I never wanted to talk about it," she confessed, "because I didn't want anyone to know. They told me she was, you know, not right in the head. I thought maybe someday that would happen to me." I wanted her to go on, to tell me as much as she knew about what happened, but I was having trouble formulating questions that wouldn't embarrass her, so I simply sat and listened, hoping she would go on talking. She did. The story she told me was the sort one only reads about in books of fiction.

When my mother was a small child growing up in Detroit, her divorced mother, Lila West, ran a boarding house in order to make a living. The establishment became a "blind pig" during Prohibition, illegally distributing alcohol. Lila didn't want her daughter exposed to the type of people who might patronize such a place, so she decided it would be in Ernestine's best interest to send her to live with her grandmother on a farm in Missouri.

My mother loved life on the farm, attended school, and got to know members of the community. She was acquainted with two boys, the Schamel brothers, who died while under the care of her grandmother. The boys' mother had died and they were being raised by their father. When they became sick, as my mother remembered it, Mr. Schamel brought them to Bertha Gifford, who was known in the area as a "volunteer nurse." When individuals in the community became ill, they were brought to her and she cared for them until they either recovered—or died. Because of her status as "nurse," autopsies were never performed on the deceased; the doctor in town would simply sign the death certificate.

As my mother related these stories from her hospital bed, she said she thought that, if her grandmother had intentionally been responsible for the deaths of the Schamel brothers, it was probably because she felt sorry for them, growing up without a mother.

There was another man my mother vaguely remembered who had purportedly died at the hands of her grandmother.

"But he was the town drunk," she stated emphatically, as if to offer her statement as a defense.

In my mother's recollection of events, Bertha Gifford had been accused of poisoning "four or five" people, had gone to trial and then had later been sent to the state mental hospital. What little my mother knew about what had happened consisted of fragments extracted mostly from relatives who were shamed into silence after Bertha had been incarcerated. There had been one other source, but she was unable to make use of it when she found it: Back in Detroit months after her grandmother's arrest, ten-year-old Ernestine opened up the Sunday *Detroit Times* to look for the comic strip pages. Inside the newspaper was a drawing—a caricature—of a shifty-eyed woman in a nurse's smock and cap who was depicted slipping a bottle of poison into her pocket. The feature story detailed the trial of Bertha Gifford. Without reading any of the text of the article, Ernestine ran to her mother with the paper in her hand.

"She took it away from me and told me never to talk about it again," she told me. Her mother lived another sixty-three years past that event; the two never spoke of it again.

"If we could find that newspaper, we could find out what happened," my mother told me that night, and her words made me realize that, for all the years that had gone by, she had never known the truth: Had her beloved grandmother, who had been so kind to her, really murdered innocent people? Or had it been a mistake, a witch hunt perhaps, on the part of ignorant country folk? For well over half a century, she had lived with these questions unanswered.

"I want you to look into it," she told me. "Do some research and see what you can find out."

I assured her that I would at my first opportunity. Then I kissed her on the cheek and left. For the hour that it took me to drive home, my thoughts revolved around how I would find answers for her.

Chapter Two
Precursors to a Criminally Insane Mind

The danger in dragging the skeleton out of the closet to have a closer look at it is that when you do, you may discover that, in some ways, it resembles you.

My mother's confession regarding what she knew of my great-grandmother created a nucleus of energy in my brain around which a myriad of thoughts continued to whirl. Mom's close bond with her grandmother had been severed by Bertha's arrest and subsequent incarceration. That bothered me. I was curious to know what had ultimately happened to her, how she had lived out her days. Mom knew little of what had happened to her after her trial, and that saddened me.

I wondered, too, if my mother's reluctance to disclose the information had somewhat to do with her trepidation about the deeply sensitive, sometimes brooding aspect of my personality. She had told me that night in the hospital how she had always feared that her grandmother's alleged insanity would manifest itself in her someday, that it might be passed down genetically somehow. Perhaps she had quietly observed the melancholy, reclusive tendencies in my own nature and had worried that these characteristics were precursors to a criminally insane mind. I was less concerned with my mother's reasoning than I was with the rationale behind Bertha's actions—if, in fact any of this was actually true. I tried to keep in the back of my mind the truth that Mom was ten years old when all this allegedly happened, and our minds have a way of selectively recalling our own histories. Still, I searched for answers, tumbling these thoughts around in my mind like old runes in the hands of an archeologist.

Several weeks after my mother's disclosure, I had occasion to visit a local campus of the University of California. As I waited for a friend, I ducked into the campus library, and while there I noticed the index to the *New York Times*. My great-grandmother's arrest had occurred in 1928. I pulled out the volume that contained references for that year. *What are the chances...?* I thought. If it had been a big enough news story, it certainly would have made the *New York Times*. When I found "Gifford," the first entry under that name read as follows:

GIFFORD (Mrs.), Bertha—arrested on charge of poisoning E Brinley and E Schamel.

The date of the issue referenced was August 26th.

In 1928 my great-grandmother had been written about in the *New York Times*. The validity of it overwhelmed me. Suddenly this strange story I had been told by my mother had become fact, had become history. I scrambled up to find the microfilm room.

In minutes I had located several tall metal file cabinets marked "New York Times" with their long, shallow drawers labeled by year. I slid open the drawer for 1928, found the box stamped "August 15-26" and headed for a machine.

I scanned slowly through the August 26 issue—until the word "poisoner" caught my eye.

The headline read, "**HELD AS POISONER AFTER DEATH OF FIVE.**" I must have sat in front of the microfilm reader for twenty minutes, staring at the story, reading it again and again. It was just as Mom had said. The article stated that her grandmother had indeed poisoned five people. My mother's speculation was that Bertha had done so as some sort of mercy killing. But Bertha's defense seemed to be that she herself took some poison as "medicine" and had not intended to kill anyone. Was it possible that she had been innocent, that, in her rural farmwife way of life, she had tried to help these people but had unintentionally, ignorantly, taken their lives instead?

I was immediately consumed with the thought of an extensive investigation. All the romantic ideas of solving a sixty-five-year-old mystery and exonerating my great-grandmother filled my head—and my heart.

My mother was ten years old when Bertha was arrested. How must it have been for that little girl to watch a stranger come and take her beloved grandmother away? And then to be whisked back to her mother in Detroit, with no explanation given, and none of her questions answered—not then, not ever. As long as her mother was alive, she had refused to talk about it. All these years, she had never known any of the details of what had really happened. No one had ever told her the truth. Had her grandmother been a victim of false accusations? Had she been found guilty despite her innocence? Or had she been some homicidal monster who deserved to be locked up for her cold-blooded, torturous murders?

How my mother had lived with these questions all her life, I could not fathom. As for me, I had to know the truth.

I don't remember anything about lunch with the friend I'd come to meet that day. I do remember being extremely distracted, unable to really focus on anything other than getting home to call my mom. When I did, and told her what I'd found, she was quiet. At the time, I didn't understand why. Looking back now, I am aware of the unresolved emotions that were stirred in her.

We talked for some time on the phone about what the next step in the investigation should be. Despite her somber mood, Mom was determined to go forward and do what we needed to do to find more answers. I was certain that local newspapers were the key to the details of the story. But "local" to the small town of Catawissa where Bertha had lived was eighteen hundred miles from us. I proposed that we travel to Missouri in the summer, when I would have time off from school. It seemed a wild idea to me when I said it, yet Mom readily agreed, and within the week she had purchased airline tickets and was making travel arrangements.

Chapter Three
A Prescribed Behavior

Hindsight is everything, of course. Had I known what horrific discoveries I was about to make, I would have planned our trip differently. I would have gone alone. As it was, I let Mom spend her time booking motel rooms, making rental car reservations, and planning our itinerary while I filled my days teaching school, grading papers, and looking forward naively to what I thought would be a week away from the stress of everyday life.

We went in August, the weekend after summer school ended. Mom had booked a red-eye flight from Ontario International Airport that would set us down in St. Louis at around six o'clock on a Monday morning. From there we would pick up a rental car and drive to our motel in Frontenac, a community just outside the city.

As we boarded the plane, we both noticed a tall, fresh-faced kid in an army uniform who looked lost and alone. Mom said hello to him as we passed him in the aisle. He turned in his seat to ask where we were going. My mother is an army veteran, so they had enough in common to engage in pleasant conversation for awhile. (Of course, Mom told him we were 'going to visit the place where she grew up,' never revealing our true motive for traveling to Missouri. This would set the pattern for her response during our trip. Whenever someone asked why we were visiting, she would tell them something innocuous, and would quickly become furious if I began to talk about her infamous grandmother.) They were still talking as I drifted off to sleep after take-off. As I recall, their conversation was the last pleasant experience we had for some time.

Blessed with an uncanny ability to sleep almost anywhere, I dozed for most of the flight. Mom was not so fortunate. By the time we landed, she was tired and irritable, having slept very little. She wanted only to get to our motel so she could sleep comfortably for a few hours before our adventure began in earnest. (She had made arrangements for an early check-in.) We were hungry, too, so we decided we would pick up the rental car, get a big breakfast somewhere, then check in at the motel.

Except that when we arrived, our room wasn't ready. We'd gotten to the motel just as many others ahead of us were checking out that morning, so we waited a half hour, only to be told the room would not be ready "for a couple of hours." Mom was livid. She was seventy-six years old and she was tired and she had put a great deal of thought into her planning so that we would be, as much as possible, physically comfortable. In my travels, I have learned that oftentimes things don't go according to plan. Part of the adventure of life for me is drifting where the wind serendipitously takes me. Alas, my poor mother does not share my world view—or at least she didn't at that moment.

It would have helped things if I had been a bit more sensitive to her frustration with the management of the motel and with her need to rest. My mindset was one of discovery, however; I just couldn't wait to get to a library.

I asked the clerk at the front desk the location of the nearest public library. Then somehow I convinced Mom that we should make use of our time while we waited for our room by checking to see if the *St. Louis Post-Dispatch*, the large metropolitan newspaper of the area, had carried any stories about Bertha during the time of her trial. I was also curious to find out if a Missouri library would hold copies of the *Detroit Times* on microfilm, as I was determined to find the issue Mom had seen when she was a child. I was particularly intrigued by it because Mom remembered in detail an illustration that ran with the article, a drawing of a woman in a nurse's smock hiding poison in her pocket. She seemed sure in her recollection that the title read, "Bertha Gifford—the Lucretia Borgia of Franklin County, Missouri."[1]

We found the library quickly and at my inquiry, the reference librarian informed us that, no, they did not have the *Detroit Times* for that era. They did, however, have the *St. Louis Post-Dispatch* for the 1920's and '30's. Since we knew from the *New York Times* article that Bertha had been taken into custody on or about August 26, 1928, I didn't bother looking in an index. I simply loaded the microfilm for that date onto the machine in hopes that there might be an article about her arrest.

I hadn't expected it to be front page news.

---

[1]During the Italian Renaissance, Lucretia Borgia, daughter of Rodrigo Borgia (Pope Alexander VI), was married several times and was said to have had countless lovers. It has been rumored down through the ages that she poisoned many of her lovers with powdered foxglove (digitalis) dropped into their wineglasses from a ring she wore.

Chapter Four
"To Quiet Their Pains"

WOMAN CONFESSES GIVING POISON TO
THREE PERSONS WHO DIED IN HER HOME

This was the headline that leaped out at us when we found the front page of the *St. Louis Post-Dispatch* for August 26, 1928. As I recall, both Mom and I made some exclamatory remarks simultaneously which don't bear repeating.

We were already aware, from the *New York Times* article, that Bertha had made a statement of some sort saying she had given the victims arsenic. It wasn't the content of the headline that shocked us; it was the size and scope of it. Somehow, since the story had been kept hushed up in my mother's family for years, we had assumed there had been little publicity. We were wrong. Her arrest and trial were written about extensively. The gist of the first article was this:

When Bertha was arrested on August 25, she was charged with the murder of Edward P. Brinley, but she was suspected of having been involved in the deaths of at least four others. They were: Sherman Pounds, Beulah Pounds, Lloyd Schamel and Elmer Schamel.

After being taken into custody, Bertha made a written statement to Chief of Police Andrew McDonnell that, on three separate occasions, she had added arsenic to medicine that had been prescribed for Lloyd Schamel, his brother Elmer, and Edward Brinley. According to the newspaper article, she stated:

I, Bertha Gifford, wife of E. B. Gifford, now living near Eureka, Mo., hereby state of my own free will, without threat or promise of immunity, that my husband and I lived in the Nicholson place, near Catawissa, about August 8, 1926, when George Schamel brought his son Lloyd, 8 or 9 years old, and his son, Elmer John, about 7, to our house where he and they made their home with us. Lloyd was sick at the time. Dr. Hemker waited on him and left some medicine for him. I put some arsenic in the medicine before I gave it to him, and Lloyd died on or about Aug. 11, 1926. About Sept. 18, 1926, Elmer John Schamel took sick. Dr. Hemker was called and left some medicine for him, and I put some arsenic in it, and Elmer John died about Sept. 22. About May 15, 1927, Edward Brinley about 48 years old, drove up to our house in an old Ford. He was drunk. He came in, sat down for a little while, then got up and went out and fell down on the concrete walk. My husband went out and brought him in and fixed the bed for him in the front room and my husband laid him on the bed. His mother came over and insisted we call a doctor. So I called Dr. Hemker. He left some medicine for him and I put some arsenic in the medicine. He died May 16, 1927. In all three cases the patients were suffering from severe pains in the stomach and I put arsenic in their medicine to quiet their pains.

This statement was referred to repeatedly as a "confession," but I couldn't see that Bertha was confessing to anything beyond trying to foolishly augment the doctor's orders with a bit of folk medicine. It is important to note here that no autopsies had been performed on these individuals when they died. They were sick, they had been under the doctor's care, they died, and they were buried. End of story—for the time being.

The Post-Dispatch article went on to give further details regarding the circumstances of the alleged victims' deaths.

In December of 1922—five years before Ed Brinley died—the Giffords' elderly relative and neighbor, Sherman Pounds, paid them a visit. Within hours of arriving he suddenly became ill and died. His death had never been explained.

Two years later, Sherman Pounds' seven-year-old granddaughter, Beulah, came to the Gifford home for a visit. She died the next day.

The Schamel brothers died in the late summer of 1925. At that time, Gene had asked their father, George Schamel, to come and stay at the farm while they did some work together. (The Giffords had employed Schamel in this way many times over the course of several years.) George, a widower, had brought along his boys, Lloyd, nine, and Elmer, seven, as there was no one to look after them at home. While the Schamels stayed with the Giffords, Bertha would tend to them. The night the family arrived at the Giffords', Lloyd became very ill, complaining of a stomach ache. (This account conflicts with Bertha's statement that Lloyd was sick when he arrived.) He died two days later. One month and eleven days later, Elmer also became ill suddenly, and died within a few days.

Eight months later, in the spring of 1927, Ed Brinley died at the Gifford home. Brinley, formerly a butcher who had lost his job, often did odd jobs for the Giffords. The night before his death, he had collapsed outside the Giffords' farmhouse. He was brought in and placed in the guest bedroom to sleep it off, but he became ill the next day and later died.

In each of these cases, the doctor who signed off on the death certificates was Dr. W. H. Hemker, who had been practicing medicine in the community of Catawissa for twenty-six years. The cause of death each time was listed as "unknown—acute gastritis and toxic condition contributory." No post-mortems were ever done—until Ed Brinley died. "For several years," the article noted, "it has been neighbors' gossip that there was 'something queer' about the 'House of Mystery.'" Ed Brinley's widow, Ludelphia, incensed at his sudden death, asked the chief of police to investigate. Subsequently, Mrs. Gifford had been indicted for the murder of Ed Brinley.

Mom had said she thought her grandmother had been accused of "four or five" murders. And here they were. Nothing we had read in the article pointed to the deaths as being "mercy killings," as my mother had always wanted to believe. But certainly that aspect would have emerged during the trial. For now, it was validating just to have found documentation. The sense I had, sitting there in that library so many miles from home, squinting to read the badly photocopied newsprint on the screen of the microfilm reader, was that we had gone to the attic together and discovered a long forgotten trunk, and then found within it a bundle of letters. We had just read the first one. Little did we know, there were many more to come. Each one would give us further insight into an event that had happened more than half a century before. But sometimes we would have to read between the lines.

Two further statements in the Post-Dispatch article were chilling. The first was the account of Bertha having been taken into custody by Chief McDonnell (who had been called into the case "because of his reputation as a shrewd detective"). When police came for her, the article states, she made no protest or verbal response: "Quietly she placed a black hat on her graying hair, pulled on a light coat over her blue house dress and got into the machine with McDonnell." The image corresponded with a detailed account my mother had given me of Bertha's arrest.

The other statement that leapt off the page was the last line of the article: "Mrs. Gifford is 50 years old and is the mother of a 15-year-old boy and a 10-year-old girl." The statement is not quite accurate; the "10-year-old girl" was not her daughter, it was her granddaughter—my mother.

Chapter Five
"I Want to Tell the Truth."

As a general rule, one reel of microfilm can contain as many as seven to ten issues of one newspaper. After we had printed out and read through the first article, I continued scrolling through the reel to find the following day's edition, in case it might contain a follow-up story. It did. The headline for August 27 read: "**CONFESSED POISONER SILENT ON SIX DEATHS.**"

This time the page included a photograph of the Schamel brothers sitting side by side, each holding a puppy. The caption read: "Lloyd and Elmer Schamel, killed with arsenic while they were living in the home of Mrs. Bertha Gifford." The six deaths mentioned in the headline were in addition to the three which had been detailed in Bertha's "statement." The article began as follows:

> Awaiting arraignment, Mrs. Bertha Gifford, who admits poisoning three persons, shed her mask of bravado today and wept.
>
> The rather plump farm woman of 50, who faced Chief of Police Andrew McDonnell of Webster two days ago with sun-burned arms akimbo, confessing she had given arsenic to two children and a man staying in her Catawissa home, all of whom later died, tearfully berated McDonnell because newspapers printed her confession yesterday.
>
> Sheriff Arthur Gorg and McDonnell questioned her as to six other deaths in the two-story frame

dwelling on the Bend road, between Pacific and Catawissa, which caused it to become known to neighbors as the "house of mystery," but she declined to add to that confession.

Covering her face with a blanket, she repeated her explanation of the three murders—that she put arsenic in the medicine of the two children—Lloyd and Elmer Schamel, and in that of Edward Brinley, a friend and neighbor, because they were suffering and she wanted to "quiet their pains."

She has refused food since Saturday night, and although on the verge of collapse, she has refused to see a doctor.

I was trying to exercise best practices in terms of my journalistic nature, but perhaps I was beyond objectivity at that point. It just seemed to me, again, as if the reporter had indulged himself with some pretty heavy-handed editorializing. I could understand Bertha's anger toward Andrew McDonnell; he had asked for her statement and she'd given it, then he'd characterized it as a confession, shown it to the press who'd made it public to her family, friends and neighbors, then clapped her in jail. I'd be a bit out of sorts about all that, too. I might even lose my appetite, if it began to look as if I might be facing a hangman's noose in the near future.

As this next article went on to explain, authorities were now investigating accounts of other deaths in addition to Sherman and Beulah Pounds, the Schamel brothers and Ed Brinley—many other deaths.

In 1917, James Louis Ogle, a hired man who worked for the Giffords, died while in Bertha's care. Two weeks prior to his death he had been diagnosed with malaria by Dr. Hemker and was being treated for that condition. When he developed gastritis, Hemker assumed it was as a result of the malaria. Here again, no autopsy was performed following the death, even though he died in the Giffords' home. It was simply assumed that he had died from complications related to the malaria.

Between the deaths of Ogle and Sherman Pounds, a three-year-old girl who was unnamed in the newspaper account became sick almost immediately after arriving at the Giffords for a visit. Dr. Hemker was called but the child died a few minutes after he arrived. (I would learn much later that this child was also related to the extended Pounds family, was also named Beulah but was not identified by name in the paper out of deference to her mother; she was born out of wedlock.)

Bertha Gifford's own mother-in-law, Emilie Gifford, was in her late sixties in 1912 when she came to stay with her son and daughter-in-law. She became ill the night she arrived and died while there. The cause of death was listed as "organic heart trouble" on the certificate of death.

A year and a half later, James Gifford, the younger brother of Gene Gifford, died while staying with his brother and sister-in-law. He was thirteen years old. The cause of death was listed as "whooping cough." (That same year, Gene and Bertha had a son together. They named him James.)

By the time Edward Brinley died a dozen or so years later, Dr. Hemker had become suspicious; Brinley's symptoms were similar to those of others who had suddenly taken sick and died under Bertha's care, and a familiar pattern had emerged that he could no longer overlook. After Brinley's death, Hemker consulted a colleague in Pacific. The doctors could not agree on whether Brinley had been intentionally poisoned, so Dr. Hemker finally signed off on the death certificate.

And he did nothing else to investigate his suspicions. Though he could have insisted upon an inquest or at the very least, an autopsy, in each case, he did not. But when the press began to question his rationale, he claimed that he never acted for fear of reprisal. He expressed his concern that the Giffords would sue him for libel. "Suppose I was wrong," he said. "I didn't want to lay myself open." It seemed that he had reason to be afraid. When Ludelphia Brinley finally succeeded in getting prosecuting attorney Frank Jenny to investigate the death of her husband Ed, a grand jury convened and listened to testimony from several witnesses, including relatives of Brinley, relatives of the Pounds, George Schamel and Dr. Hemker. Immediately, Bertha Gifford threatened libel suits against any neighbors who testified and against any newspapers that would report on the hearing. The investigation had been called off—"scared off," is how it was characterized in the press. Bertha Gifford was a fifty-four-year-old gray-haired woman who stood only five feet two inches tall. Apparently, she was quite an intimidating force.

But not intimidating enough. In the months following the grand jury presentation, community members continued to talk among themselves and as they did, new witnesses emerged. Popular sentiment against her grew and pressure on authorities increased until they finally gave in; a second grand jury investigation was called eight months after the first one. This time, Jenny produced evidence that seemed to show a correlation between the time periods of some of the deaths and Bertha Gifford's signatures in the log books of two separate drug stores—for the purchase of arsenic. Each time, Bertha had claimed she was buying the poison to rid her barn of rats. Each time, someone had died not long afterward. Several weeks later, the grand jury brought back two indictments for first degree murder, and Bertha Gifford was taken into custody.

When Chief McDonnell had finished taking Bertha's statement, he explained to her that it might be used against her. She nodded, indicating that she understood, and told him, "I want to tell the truth. I told you about giving some of them arsenic. Maybe I gave some others arsenic, too."

Despite the August heat that had permeated the small library that day, this statement sent a cold chill through me. What kind of woman was this? I suppose all along I had been hoping to find that she was simply dim-witted or slightly addled or well-intentioned but skewed in her reasoning—slightly irrational, perhaps, but not a vicious killer. The evidence was beginning to point toward the latter. The question began to burn in me: What kind of woman *was* she?

Chapter Six
"Sickbeds and Funerals"

In 1874, nine years after the Civil War ended, Bertha Alice Williams was born in Morse Mill, Missouri, a tiny community southwest of St. Louis. She married young to a man by the name of Henry Graham. They had one child together, a daughter, Lila—my grandmother—who later had one child, a daughter—my mother.

From all accounts, Henry and Bertha Graham lived the quiet rural farm life in Morse Mill—until Gene Gifford came to town.

When Eugene Gifford met Bertha Graham, he was a young man of twenty—and she was a married woman of thirty. My mother has always told me that her grandmother was considered attractive. ("People said she was beautiful.") At five feet, two inches tall, she was petite in her youth, with auburn hair and blue eyes. Though I never knew my great-grandmother, I did know my grandmother…and I know my mother. These are women with strong personalities and a certain subtle wildness, a smoldering edge which could burn intensely at times. Whatever it might have been, Gene saw something in Bertha that drew him in pursuit of her—in spite of her marital status, the age difference between them, and the wagging tongues of a small town.

Previously, rumors had been circulating around Morse Mill that Henry Graham had been unfaithful to his wife. With her husband's infidelity as her rationale, Bertha began to spend more and more time with Gene openly, caring little who knew or what was said about the affair. Eventually, she quarreled with her husband over it. Some months later, Henry fell ill with pneumonia and died shortly thereafter.

Bertha collected his life insurance money and it served as a dowry for her marriage to Gene less than a year later. The couple left Morse Mill and settled in Catawissa, a relatively short distance away with today's fast cars and well-maintained roads, but perhaps far enough away in those times to get a fresh start with new neighbors. Catawissa is little more than a broad strip of land along the Meramec River where farmers have congregated to plant crops in the rich earth. When the Giffords arrived, there were several other farms, a general store, a post office, and an old school house that was built in 1871.

Described in newspaper accounts as being "a smooth-shaven man of medium stature with a ready smile," Gene Gifford made his living by leasing out farms in Jefferson and Franklin Counties. He "kept good cows" and had several teams of mules with which he worked the land, growing corn and raising hogs. Corn is a versatile crop. Gene apparently used it not only for human consumption and to feed his hogs but as a basis for the "moonshine" he brewed. In 1926, a still was found on the farm he was leasing. He was found guilty of violating the "bone dry law" and ordered to pay a five hundred dollar fine. His criminal record did not seem to diminish him at all in the eyes of the community; Gene was an affable, easy-going man who was well-liked and well-respected.

In fact, even when sentiment in the community began to turn against Bertha, especially after the grand jury indictments, many people were sympathetic toward Gene, who seemed genuinely baffled by all the scandal. He insisted on his wife's innocence, reiterating again and again his statement that she was "nervous" and prone to high blood pressure, and those conditions had led her to make her statement to Chief McDonnell. It was Gene who, upon Bertha's arrest, immediately retained counsel in the person of Attorney W. L. Cole.

One of my mother's most vivid childhood memories is that of her grandmother's arrest. It was a hot August day, in the late morning hours. She and Jim (Bertha and Gene's son, my mother's half uncle) were sitting outside in the shade of a large tree in the front yard. In the quiet of the heavy air, they watched a car coming slowly up the road, then were surprised when it pulled into the circular driveway. A man got out and asked for Mrs. Gifford. Jim went into the house and brought his mother to the door. Words were exchanged that my mother didn't hear, though she tried to eavesdrop, and then everyone moved into the house, including my mother, who followed her grandmother into her bedroom.

"She was always vain about her looks," Mom has told me many times. "She didn't want to leave the house without powdering her face." Later newspaper accounts depict her as stopping to put on a hat, which she apparently did, but Mom has said that Bertha's primary concern at that moment was making sure her cheeks were rouged and her face looked presentable.

Meanwhile, Jim had run down to a lower field to bring Gene back to the house. There were a few words exchanged between the adults, Gene made a brief phone call, no doubt to make arrangements for the care of the children, then Bertha walked calmly out of the house with Chief McDonnell, got in his car, and they drove away.

It may seem that she was astonishingly poised for someone who was being arrested on a murder charge, but in fact, Bertha had no idea she was under arrest. Although she and Gene were fully aware of the testimony given at the grand jury hearing, they had still been awaiting the outcome. Chief McDonnell did not announce Bertha's arrest when he arrived at the farm. Instead, he offered the pretext of wanting to "talk to" her about her role in the deaths of Ed Brinley and the Schamel boys. She agreed with him readily as she was more than willing to take the trip to town to give her side of the story. She had no idea when she left that day that she would be spending that night—and many nights—in the Franklin County courthouse jail. In fact, according to McDonnell, Bertha told him on the drive into Union, "I guess the neighbors have been telling you a lot of lies about me. My husband and I expected that," then asked him if he would be keeping her in the jail overnight. He refused to answer her.

Andrew McDonnell stated in an article he wrote for *Inside Detective* magazine in 1935 that he was asked by Frank Jenny, the prosecuting attorney, to go out and bring Bertha Gifford in for questioning with the hope of gaining a confession from her. By Jenny's own admission, the case against Bertha was "very weak," because there was no motive for the murders and very little evidence, except that the individuals had died while under Mrs. Gifford's care. Further complicating the case were the conflicting reports of Bertha's neighbors; while some had their suspicions, others still referred to her as the "angel of mercy" who had nursed their loved ones during illness, a woman who would drive "ten miles over bad roads in wintry weather to offer her services."

It was Frank Jenny's hope that Andrew McDonnell would coax a confession out of Bertha, thus making a conviction much more probable. McDonnell, with a classic cops-and-robbers style, agreed to go out and bring her in. His method of successfully extracting the "truth" from her? He simply left her waiting in his office all day, alone, "doing a lot of thinking." When he returned, he found that "her thoughts apparently hadn't been any too good company," because she immediately began to talk about "what folks are saying." She went on to tell him that the neighbors had been upset with her ever since little Beulah Pounds had died, but that she hadn't given any arsenic to Beulah, only Brinley and the Schamel boys. When McDonnell asked her why, she told him she took it herself to slow her heart rate down when it beat too fast. "I wish I had some now," she told him. He merely listened to her story—then had her taken to a jail cell. The next morning she signed the statement which was immediately publicized as her confession.

Chapter Seven
"The Two Pictures of Mrs. Gifford"

Bertha's court date was eventually set for November 19th, which meant that she would be incarcerated for two and a half months, waiting to go to trial. During this time, Gene visited her every day, driving the slow and winding fifteen miles out from the farm to the jail in Union.

At first, she refused to eat. For five full days she rejected any food brought to her, drinking only water. She became withdrawn and would speak only to Gene and the sheriff assigned to the courthouse, Sheriff Gorg; if others approached her, she climbed onto her cot and covered herself completely with a blanket. She spent her days sitting quietly, sometimes talking to Gene, then at night would pace the floor of her cell, crying and moaning. Finally, Gene brought her some ice-cream and coaxed her into eating it. After that, she began to eat a little bit each day. By the time the trial began, however, she had lost a considerable amount of weight.

Meanwhile, rumors swept like crows from farm to farm. The *St. Louis Post-Dispatch* reporter characterized Bertha as "a soft-spoken woman inordinately fond of attending sickbeds and funerals." Neighbors came forward wanting to testify to her morbid fascination with death and dismemberment—and the newspaper quickly printed their accounts:

> On one occasion, according to persons who knew
> her well, she heard a man had been run over by a
> locomotive and [she] jumped into her automobile to

drive eight miles in order to view the victim. While other women covered their eyes, she stepped boldly forward and looked at the man.

Relatives of Beulah Pounds told the story of how, after Beulah's death, they had talked about asking for a post-mortem. "Mrs. Gifford was usually a quiet woman but she certainly got mad," the little girl's aunt recalled. "She said some terrible things."

A woman named Eva Ramsey wrote a letter to Sheriff Gorg asking him to question Bertha Gifford about the death of her daughter, Mary Elizabeth Brinley, in 1925. The seven-year-old child had undergone surgery while suffering from a "spinal infection." When she was released from the hospital she was taken to her grandmother's farm in Catawissa to convalesce. Mrs. Ramsey returned home but came back several days later to see her daughter.

> When I arrived, I learned that Mrs. Gifford had been sitting up day and night with Mary Elizabeth. The night before her death my sister saw Mrs. Gifford bending over the baby's bed. She had a little medicine box in her hand. When my sister spoke to her she put that box back in her apron pocket in a hurry. My baby died the next day.

The account in the Post-Dispatch continued:

> Mary Elizabeth was always afraid of Mrs. Gifford. When she was looking after the baby, Mrs. Gifford would come to the table for a meal and never speak a word. She'd swallow a few mouthfuls of food and then hurry right back to the baby's bed. It looked like she couldn't take her eyes off the sick baby, they said. My sister told me to get the baby away from her and I thought of taking the child somewhere else. But the next day the baby died.

Mary Elizabeth's father, Caswell Brinley, had also had Mrs. Gifford 'sit up' with him. Some time after his daughter's death he was severely injured in a car accident. He was taken first to a relative's home where he spent the night, then to a hospital the next day. While he was in the relative's home, Bertha received the news of his accident and rode several miles on horseback to sit by his bedside through the night. Several days after he was taken to the hospital, he died.

Many of the accounts of Bertha's involvement in sickbed deaths surfaced during the second grand jury hearing. Apparently during the time in which the court heard testimony, a steady stream of farmers and their wives and loved ones came forward to recount stories of sudden death. Two of those individuals who appeared before the court at that time were Mr. and Mrs. George Stuhlfelder. Three of their children had died while being tended to by Mrs. Gifford.

"We did not think there was anything strange about the death of our children until this investigation was begun," Mrs. Stuhlfelder said. "Everybody in this part of the country knows that Mrs. Gifford had a wide reputation as a nurse. She was thought to be a sort of Good Samaritan. Whenever anybody got sick she went to see them and helped with the medicine and helped to take care of them."

The children—Irene, seven; Margaret, two and a half; and Bernard, fifteen months—had succumbed to illnesses over an eight-year span, beginning with Bernard's death in 1915. He'd had pneumonia and was under a doctor's care. Bertha heard of it and came over, telling Mrs. Stuhlfelder to go on about her chores, and she would take care of the toddler. That night he started to vomit—and continued vomiting for four days until he died. In 1921, Margaret also came down with pneumonia and was under Dr. Hemker's care. Again, Bertha came to the house, this time telling Mrs. Stuhlfelder, "The baby looks to me as if she's awfully sick. I don't think she'll get well." Not long afterward Margaret began to vomit. She died three days later. Irene, the oldest child, had been plagued with stomach problems. After Dr. Hemker prescribed some medicine for her, she began to improve rapidly. Then Bertha came by. Hours later Irene began to vomit. She was sick for nine days before she died.

The children were not the only victims in the Stuhlfelder family. George's mother had died while being cared for by Bertha. The seventy-four-year-old woman had come down with influenza. Again, Dr. Hemker was called to the house. Mary Stuhlfelder had been sick for a week, but finally began to recover her strength, telling her son that she felt better. Mrs. Gifford came over to sit with her, and late that night she ushered George Stuhlfelder's brother and son out of the room, telling them she had to give Mary her medicine. Within moments, the elderly woman was complaining of stomach cramps. She lost consciousness quickly thereafter and died the next day.

George Schamel testified before the grand jury regarding the deaths of his sons. He also related the story of his sister, Leona Slocum, who died a month after her nephews while she was under Bertha's care.

The name of "Grandma" Birdie Unnerstall was also brought up during the grand jury testimony. She and her son Gus had lived directly across from the Giffords—until the day that Bertha came over for a visit. Mrs. Unnerstall suddenly became violently ill and then died several hours later. This brought the tally of fatalities to seventeen.

Gus also told the story of having Bertha arrested in 1926 for "peace disturbance."

"We had a little misunderstanding," he told the court. "It was a falling out over some of Gene's property that was left in one of my sheds. I went to the Gifford place one day to talk things over and Mrs. Gifford chased me with a butcher knife and cursed me."

Was this the doting Grandma that my mother had described to me? The profile emerging was one of a sociopath, someone with no moral conscience who would kill randomly, indiscriminately. But this type of psychotic serial killer—especially a female serial killer—was nearly unheard of at that time. Could she truly be responsible for all those deaths? How significant was it that all those willing to testify against her were her own neighbors who had known her for years?

It seems there was no love lost on the part of those who came forward at the second grand jury hearing; it was more than apparent that Bertha had never been received very warmly. A background piece written by the *Post-Dispatch* correspondent quoted someone "close to the family" as saying, "Gene was always popular but people never understood Bertha. She was too peculiar. They forgave her a lot because she always helped when anybody got sick." The piece went on to describe the "two pictures of Mrs. Gifford":

She was apparently a person of two characters. Men who visited at the home of Gene Gifford, affable jesting farmer…were not much impressed with Mrs. Gifford, except as a cook. As a personality, they found her silent, colorless…. She brought in the food, waited on the table, answered in monosyllables if spoken to. A physician who attended her family regarded her as feeble-minded. And yet on one occasion she threatened a Government agent with a revolver when he was looking for a still on her farm…. The women who visited her, or who helped her cook, report without exception an opinion that she was a strong personality with a peculiar relish for stories of illness, operations, deeds of violence. She studied reports of the Snyder-Gray murder[2] and frequently regaled her kitchen audience with comment on the case as she puttered about the stove, salting the potatoes or turning the pork. She thought

---

[2] In 1927, magazine editor Albert Snyder was murdered in New York by his wife Ruth Snyder and her lover Judd Gray. The case was highly publicized.

Mrs. Snyder was "a weak fool" to confess. She did
not read books or magazines. Newspapers alone
drew her attention. She turned to a murder story as
unfailingly, say persons close to her, as a banker turns
to the financial section.

By mid-September, Frank Jenny realized that he didn't have much
more than circumstantial evidence against Mrs. Gifford, so he sought
permission to have the bodies of Ed Brinley and the Schamel brothers
exhumed. On September 18, 1928, a caravan of cars rolled out into the
bright Missouri day, stopping first at Brush Creek Cemetery to
exhume the body of Ed Brinley, extract and examine the viscera, then
moving on to the Bethlehem Cemetery near Grubville to perform the
same grim task on the bodies of Lloyd and Elmer Schamel. Frank
Jenny was accompanied by the Franklin County coroner, Dr. S. L.
Dewhirst; Dr. Ralph Thompson, a pathologist from St. Louis; Dr.
James Stewart from the state health commission; and a coroner's jury,
consisting of several local professional men (including a veterinarian)
whose job it was to observe the proceedings and later report their
findings to a judge.

Within a week, Dr. Stewart had released a statement which
revealed that the vital organs of the deceased individuals showed "no
trace of any disease," but that toxicology studies had found arsenic
present in their organs, concluding that "the persons died from
poisoning." On October 9, he presented these findings before the
coroner's jury, which confirmed the evidence, rendering it admissible
in court. Gene Gifford was present in the courtroom during the
proceedings, after which he left, chagrined, to confer with the
attorneys he had retained.

Bertha's long, hot days in jail might have overwhelmed her had it
not been for her husband's visits every day. And Gene was not the
only one to visit her. One of the last times my mother ever saw her
grandmother, she was behind bars.

After Bertha had been arrested, ten-year-old Ernestine had to return to Detroit. Her mother came down on the train to collect her and take her back. Before they left, they went to the jail to see Bertha. "My mother took me to the jail to see her," Mom told me. "There she was, behind bars, and she asked my mother if I had a good winter coat. With all the trouble she was in, she was worried about me. She wanted to make sure I had a good coat for the winter in Detroit."

Were there, in fact, two sides to Bertha Gifford? Could the loving, caring mother and grandmother that my mother had known be the same person who would slip poison to innocent men, women and children because she derived pleasure from watching them die?

Chapter Eight
A Bit More of St. Louis

By the time I had finished searching out and printing every story on Bertha Gifford from the St. Louis Post-Dispatch, we had been in the public library in Frontenac for hours, and the number of Bertha's alleged victims had grown from the handful we had expected to find to seventeen—eighteen if one suspected, as apparently many people did, that she had poisoned her first husband. And if, in fact, she had intentionally murdered all of those people, she would be eligible for the ignominious title of America's earliest known female serial killer. The thought of this both amazed and disturbed me. How could she have escaped notoriety all those years? And what did her presumed insanity foretell of my future mental health?

During those hours, I had been so immersed in the history of the case, I had been transported to another place and time. Now I suddenly realized how stiff and uncomfortable I had become. And far too late, I thought of my elderly mother. She sat slumped on a stool beside me. For a long time, she had read each story as I had found and printed it—we both had. After awhile, it had become too much to absorb and was taking too long, so we had stopped reading. I continued to print out each article, glancing at the headlines just long enough to determine that the story involved Bertha Gifford. There was extensive coverage of the trial, but we would have to read that later. We were simply exhausted—emotionally, mentally and physically.

Whenever I look back on that moment, I am plagued with guilt. My mother must have been feeling so many things, but I never stopped at the time to consider what those feelings might be. I had come in hopes of finding a story, and within hours of touching ground in Missouri, I had found an incredible one. From our concept of the volunteer nurse who had been involved in the mysterious deaths of a handful of patients, we had been brought slowly along by successive glaring headlines to the realization that Bertha Gifford, infamous in her part of the world, had been implicated in the deaths of at least seventeen community and family members. Growing up, my mother's love for her grandmother, despite the hushed family secret, had never wavered. But now she saw the woman not through a child's eyes, but from an adult point of view, and what she'd just seen didn't match her memory of the beloved grandmother who loved to cook and would go out of her way to attend to the sick. What she'd been presented with, through the words and photos in the newspaper stories, was a stranger, a severe, intimidating woman who others believed was capable of multiple murders without motivation of any kind. If I'd had the least bit more sensitivity, I would have begun to realize what those two hours in the library meant to my mom.

But I was too caught up in the thrill of our discovery. The stack of photocopied newspaper articles in my hand—the stories rich in detail and wonderfully written—constituted a window that allowed us to look back in time at a series of events that shaped our history as a family. This response may seem callous, but the fact that I was personally related to the perpetrator of these crimes still had little meaning for me; I did not think of Bertha Gifford as anyone who was "family" to me. Until recent months, I had known very little of her, had never seen her photo, never heard anyone in my family speak of her. For all intents and purposes, she was a character in an outlandish crime novel to me.

To my mother, however, Bertha Gifford had been the kind, matronly grandmother who had taken her in, given her anything she wanted, spoiled her, doted on her. In making this trip to Missouri, my mother had hoped to rediscover the noble, altruistic if misguided humanitarian who had, perhaps, taken a step too far in offering relief to those whom she had nursed. This was the mythology she had created for herself. This was how she had wanted to remember her grandmother. What she found in those newspaper reports was a psychopathic sadist who murdered indiscriminately simply for the sake of wielding her power over her victims and watching their death throes.

The intense experiences—both good and bad—which befall a child leave huge, life-long impressions, like dinosaur prints in clay, because the experiences we associate with the strongest emotions are those which become the most deeply etched into our memories. It's difficult to imagine the confusion and loss that must have swept over my mother as a ten-year-old girl who watched her grandmother leave and then later discovered that she had been arrested...and that she would never return. The loved ones in my mother's life sought to shield her from the brutal truth in its totality to protect her. But now, so many years later, in just a few hours' time, she had been presented with a horrific view of the woman who had cared for her. For sixty years, she had kept the faith of a memory and a perception which she accepted without question, but now the world as she had perceived it for so long had been irrevocably altered. Grandma Bertha was a killer.

This, I think, may be but a small portion of what my mother must have experienced that day, captive on the hard stool, slapped in the face with the evidence of her grandmother's actions.

But I didn't think of any of this as I turned to my mother after our two-hour interaction with the microfilm machine. She simply looked tired to me. And I suddenly realized how tired I was myself. We gathered our things and headed back to the motel.

This time our room was ready, and we both laid down for a couple of hours of sleep.

That night at dinner, neither of us said much. While I had been excited to discuss the newspaper stories with her, Mom seemed reluctant to talk about any of it, and I attributed this silence to her need for more rest. There didn't seem to be anything else relevant to talk about, and so I kept my thoughts to myself, sifting through them and trying to decide what I believed about this woman who, according to my mother, was loving and kind.

The next morning I was eager to hit the investigative trail, to set out in search of more information. My mother would have none of it. She wanted to drive in to St. Louis. She wanted to go to the mall.

Mom needed some time to be a tourist, to visit places she hadn't been in decades—and to feel like a normal person on vacation. Thank goodness I was at least sensitive to that. And so I did not debate our options with her. I helped her into the little white rental car and drove her to St. Louis. On the way, we listened to a Cardinals game on the radio.

Sadly, not even a baseball game and a shopping trip could ease my mother back from where she had withdrawn. She was ominously silent. We had lunch at the mall, during which she said very little. Then the plan was to shop for souvenirs. We had only gone to a few stores before she wanted to go back to the motel. She said she wasn't feeling well.

We had taken the freeway downtown and when we got in the car to return, I told her I wanted to drive surface streets because I wanted to see a bit more of St. Louis. She was irritated and impatient with this idea and had I been more thoughtful, I would have given in and driven her back to the motel using the quickest route. But I simply made light of her mood and began to follow my nose in the general direction of Frontenac—and immediately became lost. We ended up in a residential area driving down narrow streets through neighborhoods that had fallen into disrepair. Mom had been sitting sullenly, not talking.

"Where are we?" She suddenly demanded.

"I don't know," I said carelessly. "We'll find our way out and back to the highway eventually."

"Turn around!" she demanded. "You need to get us out of here! Lock your door!" I looked over at her in the passenger seat. She was terrified. I had never seen my mother like this. It was unnerving. Part of me wanted to reassure her and part of me was angry. And, as always, I was stubborn. I kept driving. She literally slid down in her seat so as not to be seen. Moments later we emerged from the residential area and found the highway again.

"Why wouldn't you turn around?" she demanded accusingly.

What could I say? The truth is that I didn't want to turn around because I wanted to drive the length of that neighborhood without incident so that I could somehow prove to her that her fears were unfounded.

"Mom, it's OK," I finally said half-heartedly. I hadn't the energy to argue the need for tolerance with her.

"No, it's not OK," she shot back. "You don't know what I know." And with that she shut down again and was silent for the remainder of the ride back to the motel.

And of course, she was right. To this day, I know very little about her personal history and the experiences that have shaped her life. From time to time she has hinted at things, and I sense that there is shame over certain events, certain relationships she has had, certain choices she has made. But she never talks about these things. So much of who she was before she was my mother is a mystery to me.

But as I drove and thought about it, I began to realize that she had reason to keep things hidden. I could see now that her mother's involvement in selling alcohol during Prohibition had been an embarrassment to her; she had alluded, at times, to the type of people who "came around" the boarding house, especially the men. These were the people my grandmother had tried to shield her daughter from, had sent her to the farm in Missouri for that very reason. And while she was an excellent student with high marks, my mother had never finished high school, dropping out to get married—the first time, not to my father—at the age of fifteen. This had been another of her long-kept secrets. I sensed that there were many more.

She had told me that she had never wanted to talk about all that had happened with her grandmother because she felt ashamed. Shame is a powerful emotion. It modifies our behavior, influences our choices. Sometimes it changes the direction of our lives because it alters who we are; if we feel that we have something to hide, we are more guarded, more reserved, less willing to open ourselves up to others.

My mother feared that other people—even her own children—would judge her for what her grandmother did, so she carried the secret with her nearly all her life. In returning to Missouri, all the shame that she associated with living here had come flooding back, and, I was sure, a thousand other memories and emotions that she simply didn't feel comfortable sharing with her daughter. Finally, I began to think more about what she was experiencing and I resolved to be more careful with her feelings.

Back at the motel room that night, I waited until she had fallen asleep, then pulled out the stack of newspaper stories so that I could read what had happened at the trial. I flipped through the pages, glancing at the bleak headlines and reading the captions below the somber photographs. Then I slid them back into the folder with our itinerary and other papers. I was simply too exhausted to attempt to decipher the many crowded columns that were filled with tiny type which had been reduced to an almost illegible size by the photocopying. They would make a good story to read later, perhaps after we returned home, when I had the time to read through them carefully.

Chapter Nine
Franklin County Courthouse

On our third day in Missouri, the day dawned gray and rainy, just as the first had.

The night before, as I had glanced over the newspaper headlines of the court proceedings, I had wondered if transcripts had been taken during the trial and if so, where we might find them. I assumed that if any existed they would reside at the courthouse—if it were still standing. Mom seemed convinced for some reason that it would be, so after a leisurely breakfast at a local café, we headed down Highway 44 toward Union, the county seat and, naturally, the location of the county courthouse.

It was easy to find. From Highway 44, we took a wide, well-maintained highway four miles in to the city of Union. As we entered the downtown area, a sign directed us to the county courthouse. A moment later we were pulling up in front of a large gray building in the classic courthouse style, with wide concrete steps leading through the portals of four Greek columns, FRANKLIN COUNTY COURT HOUSE engraved in stone across the top.

Walking into the courthouse, I was overwhelmed with the same feeling I'd had three days earlier as we'd sat in the library immersed in the newspaper stories of this woman whose DNA I carried in my body. Now the feeling was intensified. Even more than before, it was like stepping out of a time machine. All around us, people were conducting business with the court, filing legal documents, and paying traffic tickets. I felt like I was in a separate dimension as I walked among them, seeing them not only in the present but also in the past, as farmers and farmwives, gathering here to witness the much-anticipated trial of their neighbor, Bertha Gifford. My sense of the history that had so dramatically been played out here grew with each step we took.

Sixty-six years ago, my great-grandmother had been brought to this building by the sheriff. Was she restrained in any way? I doubted it. I couldn't imagine the sheriff clapping her in shackles to haul her before the court. But I could envision him helping her into the black Model A Ford—or whatever had been the official department vehicle. Did Sheriff Gorg hold her arm (just as I had held my mother's arm moments ago) as he ushered her up the steps and into this same lobby where I now stood? Or was there a back door that she would have arrived through, to go straight into the courtroom? Was Bertha led to her seat at the defense table? Or did she eschew Sheriff Gorg's escort and walk boldly in to join her attorneys? Had she been tried today, my great-grandmother would have encountered paparazzi everywhere she turned. I am certain that back then, curious onlookers waited outside on the courthouse lawn for a glimpse of her just to have a story to tell at dinner later in the afternoon.

Finding the courtroom in which Bertha's trial had been conducted was easier than I could have anticipated; we asked a general question at one of the clerk's windows and learned that the courtroom—the only courtroom—was on the third floor. For my mother, negotiating three flights of steep stairs was challenging as she'd had trouble for years with a bad knee, but she refused to take the elevator when I told her I would be taking the stairs. Slowly but surely, one step at a time, we made our way up. Arriving on the third floor, we could see a wide corridor with benches along the wall, some offices, and another clerk's window. The courtroom was directly across from the stairwell.

We opened the door and peeked inside. The courtroom was empty. We walked in and let the door close behind us.

Mom was quiet. She sat down on one of the long wooden benches in the spectator section as if she were sliding into a pew at church. I walked directly to the front to stand before the judge's bench, then turned to face the back of the courtroom. With the newspaper stories there had been photographs of this very room. I hadn't brought them and now I wished I had, but they were still relatively fresh in my mind. In more than half a century, the room had barely changed.

Mom must have said, "I don't think we're supposed to be in here" at least a half dozen times over the next quarter of an hour as I moved from one point in the room to another, staring, imagining Bertha and her attorneys at their table, the opposing counsel directly across from them, the spectator benches filled to capacity. I felt a strange compulsion to touch everything, to run my hand along the railing behind the defense table, to sit in each of the chairs, as if somehow doing so would enable me to connect with the events, the people, the words that were spoken in this room back then. Being there, seeing concrete evidence, finally, of those scenes which had formerly existed only as stories in print, began to germinate within me a sense of Bertha Gifford as a real person.

To my mother's further consternation, I began snapping pictures of everything, from every angle. While she had the sense that we were committing some unauthorized trespass for which we were about to be discovered and ejected, I was trying somehow to capture and preserve this eerie feeling of having just missed some solemn event in my family's history, arriving too late to have been a part of it but still trying to be included in some way.

I wanted desperately to take a photo of Mom sitting at the defense table, but, by then, it would have seemed callous and insensitive to ask her to pose there. I persuaded her, instead, to climb the steps to the judge's bench and sit there for a brief moment. It was enough that I talked her into doing it; I couldn't get her to smile. The resulting portrait would later be more significant than I could ever have imagined at the time.

I helped Mom down from the bench and we left the courtroom, to her great relief. There is an office for the circuit clerk there on the third floor and I stepped up to the window. I asked about transcripts for a case tried in 1928 and was told, to my disappointment, that they were recorded only if the case were appealed, which it had not been.

"Wouldn't there have been some kind of documentation of the case?" I asked. The tall, middle-aged woman smiled. She was wearing a flower print summer dress, red roses on a white background.

"Well, of course," she said, "there would have been the judgment filed. Do you know the exact date of the trial?"

I gave her the dates, and she said, "Let me go look that up" in a tone that made it seem she genuinely had nothing better to do than to search old files for us.

We waited only a few minutes until she returned with an enormous ledger cradled in her arms. She laid it down carefully on the counter between us. Grasping the front cover with one hand and holding her other hand under it for support, she gently opened the book and began gingerly turning pages.

"The paper is so old," she said, "that sometimes it begins to just fall apart. Let's see… 928…November…—ah, here it is." She found the spot and slowly rotated the book so that we could read it.

State of Missouri,————————————————Plaintiffs.
vs.
Bertha Gifford,————————————————Defendant.

All the pertinent details of the date and the place and the particulars were summed up in half a page, including the specific judgment, "wherein the defendant, Bertha Gifford, was found not guilty, by the verdict of the Jury, of murder, on the sole ground that she, the defendant, was insane at the time the offense was committed," and the court's order that she be remanded to the State Hospital "as provided for in cases of insane poor."

This was not new information to us. Mom had always known that Bertha had been declared insane and that she had been "sent down to Farmington" where the State funded hospital was located. For me, though, to whom all of this information was relatively new, it seemed amazing that here before me was a document that validated all of these crazy stories I'd been hearing. Good typing skills must have been hard to come by in 1928. Whoever had transcribed the court's judgment back then had typed "County of St. Louis" four times in the document. In each case, he or she had gone back and lined out "St. Louis" in black ink and had written in "Franklin."

"Is there a way you can make us a photocopy of that?" I asked, expecting a negative answer.

"Of course," the clerk said, smiling again. I worried, watching the dust motes float into the air as she painstakingly lifted the open book and carried it away, that she would get her nice crisp dress dirty. She returned in a brief moment, bright and clean as ever, and handed us a copy of the judgment.

Chapter Ten
"A White House with a Red Barn"

My primary reason for going to Missouri had been to facilitate the research we had done in the library and at the courthouse, but I had also wanted to see things, to get a more real sense of the picture my mother had sketched in my mind when she told me stories about the halcyon days of her life before her grandmother was arrested. What was the yard like where she and Jim had been playing? How did the house look? I asked her these questions and wondered aloud if we could find the old place now.

"The house was old when I lived there," she answered. "I doubt if it would still be there. That was a lot of years ago."

Sixty-six years had passed since she had been there. What had happened to the house since then? I was determined to try to find it. Before we'd left for Missouri, I had asked her how we would go about doing that. She didn't know. She knew the farm was near Catawissa, and she remembered that it was "a white farmhouse with a red barn," but that was all.

Catawissa is a tiny community just big enough for a gas station, a bar, a convenience store and a post office. It is located three miles southwest of Pacific. Between the two small towns there are hundreds of farms on thousands of acres, and they are linked by miles and miles of mostly paved but narrow, winding, hilly country roads. It took seeing the geographic area for me to understand why Mom held out so little hope of finding the house, even if it were still standing; we could drive up and down country roads all day looking. And how would we be sure which one it was? She had been a child the last time she'd seen it. Would she remember it?

We didn't know. But we did get lucky in one respect; that first morning in Missouri as we'd sifted through the newspaper articles, we found a line that named the road on which the farmhouse was located.

"Mom, look." I had placed my finger on the screen of the microfilm reader. "The house is on Bend road. Do you know where that is?"

She sighed impatiently. "I don't know where *anything* is."

So it was that on our fourth day, after an incredibly wonderful breakfast which included grits with maple syrup for me (a treat rarely seen on menus in Southern California), we set out for Pacific, not knowing exactly where we would go from there. We had a map of Missouri, and the tiny dot of Catawissa appears there—but none of the surrounding roads were marked.

The day had dawned cloudy again and we drove west on Highway 44 in gloomy silence. We found Pacific easily enough, as it is right off the highway. I followed the exit and we rolled slowly through the business district of the old but obviously cared for town. Now what?

I pulled into the parking lot of a convenience store.

"Where are you going?" my mother demanded. Since that first day in the library when we'd made our shocking discoveries, she had been tense and on edge, questioning every decision I made. I understood now that she was experiencing a great deal of unexpected emotional turmoil.

"I'm thirsty," I shrugged. "Want anything?"

I bought us both water—and a lottery ticket. (Later I would toss the ticket in the glove box of the rental car and forget about it. I never did check the numbers to see if we had won.) At the counter, I asked the middle-aged man at the cash register if he knew where Bend Road was.

"Oh sure," he said. "Matter of fact, you're on it. Just follow this road until it curves south—about a mile or so—then stay on it 'til you come to the bridge. Be careful now when you come to the bridge; it's just one lane. You have to pull up slowly, then make sure no one's coming from the other side before you set out across. Once you get to the other side of the bridge, you're on Old Bend Road."

I thanked him and hurried out to the car. After handing Mom her water and the lottery ticket, I drove out and headed west with resolve.

"Now where are you going?" Mom seemed to notice that I was finally driving with some sense of purpose.

"I don't know," I said, "but at least I know how to get there."

My mother replied, of course. It was not the first time in my life she had called me a smartass. And it wasn't the last.

I was just beginning to doubt the clerk's directions, to feel like we must have gone too far, when we rolled around a sharp curve and saw the bridge.

Bend Road is so called because it follows a severe curve of the Meramec River. Families who live along the road, which serves as the main link between Pacific and Catawissa, are referred to as being "from the Bend." It appears that the addition of the modifier "Old" came about when the classification of the long stretch of pavement was upgraded to "highway."

The tall bridge of iron girders which loomed before us was built in 1916. This date and the load capacity had been stamped into iron plates and welded at the top of the arc on each end of the bridge. But I didn't read or even notice that information at the time. It would be pointed out to me at a much later date. At the moment, sitting before the bridge, the small car idling lightly, I stared not up, but down, first at the long wooden planks which I would be driving across, then at what I could see of the river through the dense foliage which lined the banks and nearly obscured either end of the bridge.

"Think it'll hold us?" I asked, half joking, half terrified. My mother turned her head quickly and glared at me from the passenger seat.

"Don't be ridiculous," she snapped. I laugh to think of it now. "Ridiculous" was right. I am five foot six. At the time—even with the huge breakfasts we'd been eating—I probably topped the scale at somewhere just over one hundred twenty pounds with clothes on, including shoes. My mother is two inches shorter than I am and has a medium build. Though I didn't know it at the time, we could have rolled safely across that bridge with a good-sized elephant strapped to the top of the car—provided we weren't crushed in the process. The load capacity is twenty-five tons.

As it was, in the long moments we'd been sitting there, I had seen no other car use the bridge—which was probably just as well, since the lane is so narrow I couldn't imagine two vehicles passing each other. Because the road slopes up sharply at either end of the bridge, it is impossible to see the road on the far side before driving onto the bridge. I crept up slowly. It had begun to rain, a light but steady drizzle. I cannot say why, but I rolled my window down, perhaps to listen for the sound of a vehicle approaching from the other side. I can still hear the sound of the rain dripping through the leaves of the cottonwoods that were all around us. I started across the bridge at no more than ten miles an hour.

It must have driven my mother crazy.

"What are you doing?" she barked. "Roll up your window. You're getting the car all wet inside."

I obeyed—because now we were halfway across, and I could see that there were no cars coming from the other way. I could also see the river rolling along below us. Mom saw it, too.

"I remember this bridge," she said. Her tone had changed; she was hopeful.

The Bend bridge is a gateway into another community, separate from the town of Pacific. Talk to anyone who comes from the Bend, and they can tell you easily which years were the flood years. Heavy rains cause the Meramec to swell over her banks, filling every low area with water. Flooding makes the land fertile, though. Everything that wants to grow, does. Trees spring up like weeds and must be constantly mowed down or they will take over. Had it not been paved, the road that stretched before us on the other side of the bridge could have been a swath cut by a tractor; tall corn crowded either side of it.

We started down the road and it was almost like driving through a tunnel. For some reason, the thought crossed my mind that Gene Gifford had grown corn.

"Anything look familiar?" I asked the question more to invade my mother's silence than to garner information.

"I'm not sure," she responded reluctantly. "It all looks the same.... I mean, it's all just typical farm country." She sighed, irritated again. "I don't know, the house is a hundred years old. I don't know if it would even still be there after all these years." Then she was quiet.

We followed a curve in the road and now we could see farmhouses in the distance. The rain continued its constant accumulation on the windshield and, just as steadily, the wipers brushed it away. With the windows up, we heard nothing but the engine and this mechanical beat. For some reason we seemed to be straining to hear—what? I don't know. The voices of the dead calling, perhaps.

We rounded another curve and there was more corn. It towered over the road and I felt shut in, claustrophobic. The overcast, shadowy light and dense, humid air were oppressive. *There are ghosts here*, I began to think, when my mother's voice startled me.

"This looks familiar." She said it flatly, reluctant to trust her own memory.

"What part?" As far as I could see, the scene had remained unchanged, except for the inclusion of a new hill.

"I don't know...all of it...." She paused. "If this is where I think it is, we'll go around a bend, and the house will be there."

I was both excited and skeptical. The winding road, the corn—it all looked the same to me. What looked different to her?

"It's a white farmhouse with a red barn," she told me again. I didn't want her to be disappointed and suddenly began to feel anxious about what I would say to her if she were wrong.

I needn't have worried. The broad side of a weathered red barn was visible through the trees as we came around the curve. My foot hit the brake and we slowed quickly as I saw the tall, clean, white farmhouse standing out in contrast to the dark green trees which surrounded it.

"Is that it?" I asked quietly.

"I think so," was all she could say as she stared through the rain at the house that had been her home so long ago.

I drove down the road, turned around, and came back to pull in the gravel driveway. Mom had a fit.

"What are you doing?" she demanded.

The road dropped off on either side into deep ditches. It wasn't as if we could pull up at the curb across the street and observe the house covertly.

"I'm just trying to be safe and pull off the highway," I said. Her reaction to finding the house was the complete opposite of what I would have expected. She didn't seem to be experiencing any bittersweet moments of nostalgia. She was fearful and apprehensive.

As the car idled quietly, we sat staring at the house. It was not weathered and run down like the barn, but freshly painted and well-kept. The small front porch with its carved railings was neat and tidy. Lace curtains covered the windows. It was obvious that someone lived there, but at the moment there didn't seem to be anyone around, at least not outside.

"If this is it," Mom finally broke the silence, "the driveway curves around the back of the house, and from where it ends we'll be able to see the back porch and the cellar doors."

She seemed resolved now to know for sure, so I eased my foot off the brake and let the car roll forward slowly along the drive, the tires crunching loudly in the gravel. Just as she had said, the driveway took us to the far side of the house. There was the back porch…and the cellar doors. I stopped. A slight chill whispered through me as I peered at an upstairs window.

"People died here," I said quietly.

"Shut up!" my mother snapped. "Come on, let's get out of here."
I turned the car around and followed the drive out again, but stopped short of pulling onto the highway. When I put the car in park, Mom began to panic again.

"What are you doing?"

"I'm going to see if anyone's home." I got out before she could protest, though I could hear her saying something as I slammed the car door to keep the rain out.

I knocked repeatedly, but no one answered. Now that we had found the house, I wanted to go inside. I wanted to see the rooms and try to imagine what life had been like for Bertha—and my mother— when they had lived here.

The house number was posted in small metal letters on the wood siding of the house next to the porch. I memorized it, then hurried back to the car, got in quickly and drove out onto the highway so Mom would calm down. I knew she wasn't happy with me.

We had only gone a few hundred feet when she said, a note of surprise and familiarity in her voice, "Up there's the old schoolhouse."

I stopped in the middle of the road and looked up the hill in the direction she was pointing. Then it was finally my turn to glare at her.

"You mean *that's* the school you walked 'miles' to get to 'in the snow' with cardboard in your shoes to cover the holes?"

Suddenly she burst out laughing. "Well, it seemed really far when I was a little kid."

We needed the comic relief.

Chapter Eleven
"All the Trouble with the House of Mystery"

"I told you about the schoolhouse, didn't I?" she said.

"About how far you had to walk to get there?" I answered.

"No," she said emphatically, trying to escape from my teasing. "About how my grandmother—" She halted mid-sentence because I had stopped the car in the middle of the highway.

"Now where are you going?" she asked in exasperation as I put the car in reverse and slowly backed up. A name on a mailbox had caught my eye.

"Mom, do you remember the name 'Grodie' from those newspaper articles?" I was sure I had seen it.

"Was that name in one of the articles?" she asked, looking puzzled. "I went to school with a girl named Hope Grodie."

That was all the impetus I needed. I turned onto the gravel driveway next to the mailbox and followed its path through towering foliage—under a storm of protest from my mother. The driveway was actually a road which led past a pond and up onto a small hillock. From there I could see the house or, more accurately, the roof. I learned later that a cellar had been dug here and a foundation laid, but the house was never built, so the cellar had been turned into living quarters.

In front of us was a wooden picnic table with benches. I parked the car near it, got out and went up to the house, descending concrete stairs which were built into the ground to get to the door. I knocked, waited, then knocked again.

"Anyone home?" I called. No one answered.

As I climbed back up the steps, I saw that Mom had gotten out of the car and was sitting at the picnic table. The rain had stopped. We looked around at the trees and the pond.

"It's beautiful here," I said, sitting down beside my mother whose body drooped with the weariness of emotional overload.

"Probably no one lives here," she sighed. And as she said it, the door opened and an older, silver-haired woman emerged.

"Hello," she said smiling.

I apologized for imposing ourselves on her and explained that we had come back to the neighborhood because Mom used to live in the vicinity when she was a child. I did not explain the familial connection. I told her how we'd stopped because of the name on the mailbox.

"I went to school here with a Hope Grodie," Mom told her.

"Oh, that would be my sister-in-law," she said, "my husband's sister. I'm a Grodie by marriage. My name is Mildred Grodie but my maiden name is Kober."

It took my mother and Mrs. Grodie several minutes of conversation to establish years of birth and specific time periods. Mildred was five years younger than my mom, so they wouldn't have gone to school together, though she did attend the old schoolhouse up the road. She told us that her sister-in-law, Hope, was living in a nearby city, and offered to write down her phone number so my mother could call her. After my mother's noncommittal response, Mrs. Grodie told her how to find the number which was listed in the local telephone directory. And then the conversation took a decidedly uncomfortable turn.

"Well, if you were here in 1928," she began hesitantly, still doing the figuring in her head, "then you'd remember all the trouble with the House of Mystery…."

"It's been very nice to talk to you but we have to go now," was my mother's reply as she stood up and headed for the car. I followed her reluctantly.

"That was really a terrible time for so many of the families here," Mrs. Grodie continued on the assumption that Mom knew exactly what she was referring to. "I had an aunt and three cousins who were poisoned.... Stuhlfelder was the name...."

I stopped. The Stuhlfelders. Four of them....

"We need to go *right now*." My mother was already in the car, calling to me urgently through the window. Mildred Grodie would have been only five years old when Bertha Gifford was arrested, but she would have grown up hearing every story from every neighbor and every family affected by the scandal. She would be a goldmine of tales—real, embellished and purely fictional, no doubt.

"I'm sorry," I said to Mrs. Grodie. "My mother...hasn't been feeling well."

"Oh, I understand," she said kindly.

Getting in the car and driving away was torturous. Here was a living source of information who was warm, sociable, and willing to sit on a beautiful summer afternoon and talk about days gone by. She had lived the very history that I wanted to learn. And I had to drive away.

Mom was tight-lipped and withdrawn. When I tried to talk to her, she finally snapped at me.

"I didn't want you to tell her why we're here," she said tersely. "I'm..." she stammered, "I'm ashamed of what my grandmother did to all those people."

"Mom," I told her, "You were ten years old. You had no idea what was going on or what your grandmother was doing. You're not responsible in any way for what happened."

We followed Bend Road to the central hub of Catawissa where a tiny old post office sparked a memory for my mother.

"I used to ride my horse down here to get the mail for my grandmother," she said wistfully.

I turned the car around, and we headed back down the road toward Pacific. As we rolled past the schoolhouse again, Mom turned in her seat to face me.

"I started to tell you before about the schoolhouse."

I made some response to let her know I was listening, though it was only with one ear. I was trying to figure out how I could drop her off at the hotel and go back to talk to Mildred Grodie.

"Well, when I came out from Detroit, my grandmother went to the school board and told them, 'My granddaughter Ernestine is coming to live with me and she's going to go to school here, but this old schoolhouse is too run down and not nice enough for her. We need to build a new schoolhouse.' But I guess they weren't interested in that because they turned her down. So she went out there in the middle of the night and doused it with kerosene and set it on fire. The old schoolhouse burned to the ground, so when I came to go to school here, there was a nice new one."

She had my full attention now.

"Mom, how do you know this?"

"Oh, I heard her bragging to one of the neighbors one day. She didn't think I was listening, but I was. She used to say, 'Nothing's too good for Ernestine.' People probably didn't like her very much for saying that, but that was the way my grandmother was." She sat back in her seat. There was no shame in her tone now…only love. And pride.

The conversation gave me chills. Did Bertha Gifford really burn down the school house? Before this bit of information, I was ready to see her through the eyes of my mother. I wanted to see her that way, and I wanted to believe that my great-grandmother had herself been a victim of vicious rumor and slander, that she'd never meant to hurt anyone but was simply misunderstood in her intentions. But my mother seemed absolute in her conviction that Bertha had purposely set the fire that burned the school. If that were the case, she could easily fit the profile of someone who is disturbed, who lacks a moral compass. The story was just too outrageous to be credible anyway, and at the time I told myself that it couldn't possibly be true. My mother loved to read when she was a kid, and the story sounded like something out of gothic romance.

Long after our conversation in the rental car that day, however, I would learn that the school house did, in fact, burn down. A brief article in the April 18, 1924 issue of the Pacific Transcript mentions a mass meeting at the home of John Gifford, Bertha Gifford's brother-in-law. Community members were discussing plans for a new school house, since the old school house had burned: "The Bend school house was entirely destroyed by fire Sunday night. The origin of the fire is unknown and was discovered about half-past eleven when the flames had gained such headway that nothing could be saved." Apparently in several previous meetings, the community had voted not to spend the money on building a new school house, but now that the old one had burned, the reporter stated, "we are sure to have a new one."

The new school house would have been built in the spring and summer of 1924. Just in time for my mother to begin the first grade in the fall of that year.

Chapter Twelve
A Frivolous, Romantic Notion

I never did get back to talk to Mildred Grodie. We stopped somewhere for lunch, and as soon as we got back to the hotel, Mom started doing some preliminary packing. She was anxious to get home, but more anxious to get out of Missouri, away from the memories that had seemed to flood back and now haunted her wherever we went.

I was homesick. I missed my kids. But I wasn't ready to leave yet. I felt as if we had just dusted the surface of what there was to know about Bertha Gifford and what had happened all those years ago. I was still trying to process all the information. And I wanted to try to find more people like Mildred Grodie who had lived at the time and might be able to give us more insight into the personality of this woman.

But we had airline tickets. And Mom was more than ready to leave.

I flopped down on the bed, unsure of what to do with my time. Every morning since we'd been there Mom had talked about swimming in the hotel pool. Every day it had rained. The clouds had been clearing, though, since we'd safely rolled back over the Bend bridge, and the day, though intolerably humid, was showing a few glimpses of limited sunshine. Mom headed out to the pool—as much to have time to herself, I think, as for the benefit in terms of exercise.

When the door closed behind her, I pulled out the telephone directory and turned to the yellow pages. There were only three real estate offices listed in Pacific. I picked up the phone and called one.

The woman who answered was, like so many of the people we met in Missouri, open and friendly. I told her—well, I lied. And I've never been very good at it, so she must have been suspicious right from the beginning of the conversation.

I told her that my mother and I were from California (at least that part was true), that we'd been traveling around in the area and that Mom was thinking of moving back since she'd lived here during her childhood. We'd seen a farmhouse, I told her, out on Bend Road, and we were wondering if the current owner might be interested in selling it.

There was a pause.

"Exactly which farm was it?" she asked. I told her the address, and described the house and the barn.

"Oh, I'm familiar with the property," she said, no longer entirely friendly.

There was another pause.

I really hadn't known when I'd begun the conversation how I was going to get around to asking the name of the owner. I hadn't thought that far. I'd gone fishing without any bait and now, with my line hanging in the water, I just didn't know what to say.

"Do you know who the owner is?"

"Yes."

The conversation hung there, slack. I decided to take a more direct approach.

"Is the owner aware of the history of the house?"

"Which history are you referring to?" From her question and her tone, I knew that she knew.

"I'm related to someone who used to live in the house," I started tentatively, "someone who was accused of poisoning—"

"Oh, I know all about that," she cut me off and then proceeded to tell me nearly as much as I knew at that point about what had gone on there. She told me that the owners lived "in town" and only went out to the property on weekends. I tried to wrestle the conversation back to that one piece of information I needed.

"So the owner...." I began again.

"Oh, yes, the owner knows all about it. Everyone who lives in this area knows all about what happened back then. It's a part of our history. It's not a good part, maybe, but it's a part of it, just the same."

"So do you think he or she would—"

She cut me off again. "Oh, I wouldn't want to impose on the owner's privacy. I doubt whether they'd be willing to sell the place, but I can take your name and number and if they're interested, I'll get back to you." I gave her the information, though I didn't think I'd ever hear from her again. And as it turned out, I never did.

Minutes after I hung up the phone, Mom came back in.

"That was a short swim," I said.

"It's raining again," she said, disgusted. I looked out the window and sighed deeply.

"What were you up to while I was gone?" she asked.

I described my fruitless phone conversation with the real estate agent.

"Well, you can find out who lives there from the county recorder's office." She said this as if pretty much everyone over the age of twelve would know it. Maybe they do. At one time my mother had possessed a license to sell real estate. She knew these things. I looked at her.

"And where would we find the county recorder's office?"

"Well, it's probably right there in Union at the courthouse."

And, of course, it was.

No matter how old we get, we remain the children of our parents, and although at some point (beginning at around age fifteen, I think) we believe we know everything that they know—and then some —wc can never fully mine all the stores of wisdom that they are capable of accessing, because the truth is that as we are growing, so are they, perpetually. Still, we are amazed when they know things that we do not.

After a quick drive down the highway to the courthouse in Union, I was further amazed at how readily available this information turned out to be. The clerk took my scribbled note with the address in hand, stepped into a back room for a few quick moments, and returned with a piece of microfilm. She led us into another room, threaded the strip of film into a reader, and pointed to a name and address on the monitor. The owners of the farm were Robert and Claire Fiedler. On a scrap of paper, Mom hurriedly copied down their "town" address. The entire process, sans driving time, had taken five minutes.

Once again I was excited and Mom was chagrined.

"I don't know what you're going to do with that. We're going back tomorrow."

"I don't know what I'm going to do with it either." It was a lie. I did know. I knew exactly what I wanted to do with it but I didn't want to tell her that I felt drawn to the house somehow, that I wanted to make contact with the Fiedlers because I felt some strange connection to the house and ever since we had been there I had felt compelled to go back, to go inside and see for myself if somehow any last vestige of the past had been saved, anything that would constitute evidence of a criminal mind. I couldn't say these things to her. I couldn't tell my no-nonsense, pragmatic mother whose current agenda was to get the hell out of Missouri as soon as she could that I didn't want to leave, because I felt if I stayed just a little bit longer the time machine which had seemed to hover in the background since we'd arrived would sweep me up and transport me to 1928 and I would be able to experience what happened with all my senses, and somehow understand. It was a frivolous, romantic notion. And it filled my head to bursting.

Chapter Thirteen
"Without a Court Order"

Friday morning we awoke and began making our final preparations for departure. We would fly out in the afternoon, but we had to get breakfast, return the rental car, then get to the airport. There was still time, though. Mom left the room to get her morning coffee and once again I picked up the telephone directory. Fiedler. There were twenty-six listings. There were two listings for "Robt." But the first one had a secondary residence with a separate phone listed: "Farm, Bend Rd." I'd like to say that I hastily wrote down both numbers, but I didn't. The truth is, I tore the entire page out of the book. For a personality like mine that reveres order, this was a desecration, but a necessary one. I folded the page in half once and added it to my folder of information.

Mom came back into the room as I was still paging through the directory, looking for the state listings. I was trying to find the state hospital in Farmington, though I wasn't sure what to call it. I made a few phone calls and finally connected with a woman who explained that the "state hospital" no longer existed per se, but that I had found the "Southeast Missouri Mental Health Center," which seemed to be basically the same institution in the same location, though she assured me that it was quite different now.

I slowly, haltingly explained that I was trying to get information on my great-grandmother who had been—I stopped myself from using the word "inmate"—a patient there but had died some years ago, though when, we didn't know. She connected me to someone in the records department. I offered the same explanation.

"I'm sorry," she told me, "I can't give you any information over the phone, and even if you came here in person, you'd need a court order before we could release that information to you."

"But she must have died decades ago," I protested, "and we don't have time to get a court order. We're just here visiting from out of state, and we leave today. Can you at least tell me when she died? It would mean so much to my mother—she never knew what happened to her grandmother and they were very close. We are her last remaining descendants, and we don't even know where she's buried." I was conscious of my mother in the small room with me, her preparations suspended. She was standing a few feet away, hanging on every word of the conversation.

There was a long pause. She asked me for the name and the time period in which Bertha had resided at the "center." When I told her, she sighed heavily.

"That was so long ago.... I don't even know exactly where those records would be kept. It would take me some time to find them. And I really can't give you any information without a court order. But I will try to find out when she died and where she's buried."

"Anything you can offer us would be of help," I told her gratefully. She took my name and address, and I promised that I would pay for any photocopying that was necessary, if she would just send us what she could find. I hung up and looked at my mom.

"Well?"

"She's going to look," I said. "She's going to send me a copy of whatever she can find." But I said it with very little belief that she would.

Then we gathered up our bags, climbed into the rental car for the last time, and started on our journey back to California.

On the flight back, when I had time to review the events of our trip, something occurred to me that I had wondered about and had neglected to ask my mother.

"I'm curious about why you didn't seem to want to contact Hope Grodie," I told her. "You said she was your best friend in school."

"Well," my mother began in the tone that let me know she really didn't want to discuss the matter. "We had what you might call a falling out." She was quiet, hoping I would just let it go and wouldn't question her further.

"What happened?"

She sighed in exasperation, then told me how she had gotten into a scuffle with another girl in the schoolyard over something, she didn't remember what.

"We were fighting over something," she said, "and I pushed her down on the ground and sat on her, you know, holding her arms down and straddling her. Well, Hope saw us and she told everyone at school that…" She hesitated. "Well, she said some pretty vulgar things."

I was a bit confused. "What did she say?"

"Oh," she said, anger in her voice despite all the years that had passed, "she said it looked like I was fucking her. When I found out she said that, I was pretty mad. We were never friends again after that."

For once, I was sorry I had asked. This was obviously a painful memory, and it was one that I really didn't need to know about.

For the remainder of the flight home, I reflected on the hazards of uncovering our individual histories.

Chapter Fourteen
"Does Not Hear Strange Voices"

I was glad to be back in the arid climate of California and home to the embrace of my children, the welcome wags of my faithful dog Alex, and even the disapproving stares of my cat Calpurnia. But I still had the lingering sense that we had come home too soon. In quiet times I relived, again and again, the images of that rainy morning driving over the Bend bridge, of the tall corn and the ominous white farmhouse glimpsed through the trees. Questions still filled my mind.

On a late afternoon a few days after we returned, I paced the floor of my bedroom. In my hand was the phone directory page which had Robert Fiedler's phone number. I wanted to call. But how does one begin the conversation?

"Good evening, Mr. Fiedler, I was wondering if you knew that my great-grandmother once lived in your house and that she poisoned some people there?"

"Hello, Mr. Fiedler, you don't know me, but I'm interested in your farmhouse on Bend Road because…because…"

I didn't want to be dishonest. I wanted to be straightforward and to the point…and I could not think of a way to do that without perpetrating what amounted to a huge invasion of the Fiedlers' privacy. What if they didn't know? Was it right to reveal that people had been murdered in their house? Would it make a difference to them? How could I know without knowing what kind of people they were?

It would have been different, I suppose, if I were a different kind of person, if I were outgoing and gregarious. I am not. Introspective and reserved, I've never felt comfortable intruding upon the privacy of others. Part of me felt strongly compelled to call. Another part told me I had no right to. Finally, I opted instead to write them a letter. I sat down that night and wrote a letter introducing myself and tracing my relationship to Bertha Gifford, explaining that she used to live in the house. I asked if they would be willing to correspond with me, and I enclosed a self-addressed stamped envelope.

I put the letter in the mail the next day, hopeful. I hadn't yet decided to write about my great-grandmother—my mother seemed to be dead set against that. But my feeling of a connection with the house remained with me, and somehow I wanted to pursue it, though I didn't know why.

The letter which I had written to the Fiedlers was returned to me a week later. It was stamped "No Such Address." Perhaps they had moved. I sent the letter again, this time to the address at the farm. Again it was returned, stamped "No Such Address."

I was frustrated and disappointed but I had little time to think about such things. School had started and I had plunged back into the daily routine of teaching and grading papers by day, then going home in the evenings to maintain a household and try to raise two very different and very strong-willed teenaged boys. I had enough items to juggle; I had to let go of my obsession with unsolved mysteries in Missouri.

There is something beautiful about the month of September in California. I always associate it with the color yellow. The days are still summer-hot, but they are shorter, and the evenings cool off just enough to whisper promises of coming rain and relief from the heat in October. But the sun is still as bright as new back-to-school pencils, and the afternoon breeze rustles the leaves that will turn first golden, then brown.

I remember that it was just such a day as this in late September that I came home from work and walked down the driveway slowly to retrieve my mail. When I opened the box, along with the requisite junk mail and bills, there was a very thick legal size envelope. I pulled it out. It was from the Southeast Missouri Mental Health Center.

I hurried into the house, sat down at my desk, and sliced the letter open. Inside were nineteen photocopied pages. There was no cover letter, not even a Post-it note of explanation. But one wasn't necessary. I could see what it was right away as I began to leaf through the pages. It was Bertha Gifford's entire file, photocopied.

Somewhere there are treasures laid up in heaven, or a huge slice of good karma, served up as a reward for the kind-hearted clerk, whoever she was, who found a file that by then had been closed for forty-four years, carefully photocopied each of the nineteen pages, squeezed them into an envelope and paid the dollar and one cent postage that it cost to send it to me. The contents gave me answers to questions I would not have known otherwise.

As I sifted through the pages, the first significant piece of information I turned up was that Bertha had died from a stroke in 1951. She had lived in the institution for twenty-three years. At the very least, I would be able to tell my mother this; she had never known what had happened to her grandmother—how or when she had died. In Bertha's later years, the file revealed, she had struggled with obesity, high blood pressure and a recurring gall bladder problem—as my grandmother and then my mother would in their later years.

What captivated my attention far more than her medical history, however, was her psychiatric evaluation. The file contained an assessment which had been done initially by a Dr. Ralf Hanks. It also included the transcript of a later interview with Dr. Hanks, Bertha, and two other doctors named Tate and Hoctor. That document, in and of itself, was an amazing artifact to me as I sat staring at it in my hands. More than two pages long, single-spaced, it is a verbatim conversation, in question and answer format, between Bertha Gifford and the doctors evaluating her. For the first time, I was able to 'hear' my great-grandmother in her own defense, in her own words.

In Dr. Hanks' assessment, which was conducted in February of 1929, two months after Bertha arrived at the facility in Farmington, he observed that her "manner of speech" was "coherent, neither meager nor excessive. No flight of ideas or difficulty in thinking. No confusion and no appearant [sic] memory defect. Patient does not appear dejected nor depressed." Under the heading "Emotional status and attitude of mind," Dr. Hanks stated, "Unable to bring out any delusions or hallucinations in this examination." In his summary he said, "From information obtained from this history I am unable to make a diagnosis." In May of 1929, after Bertha had been at Farmington for five months, another notation was made in her file by Dr. Hanks: "Have been unable to find any psychosis. Nice quiet patient, good worker."

As a result of their extended interview with her in March of 1929, however, the doctors seemed to agree collectively that Bertha was exhibiting signs of psychosis; the "diagnosis agreed to" in the record is "paranoia." It's understandable how they might come to that conclusion, considering sections of the interview such as this one:

Q. "Why did they pick you out and accuse you of this?"
A. "Because they were mad at me."
Q. "What caused them to be angry at you?"
A. "My kids talking over the telephone. One of their neighbors niece was visiting them and she got to using bad language over the telephone and said it was Ernestine. Told her husband about it and he went over and told the little girl to quit, the girl told her uncle and he got mad about it and was going to kill me and my husband for saying it was her. After that they just kept on telling tales."[3]

---

[3]Note: The switch from first person to third, then back to first person again seems to have been the fault of the individual who was taking dictation for later transcription into the typed record. The same error occurs several times throughout the transcript.

"Ernestine." How strange it was to find my mother's name here, to discover Bertha implicating her somehow in all the drama that had unfolded. Was there any truth to this story? Did it have anything to do with the "bad blood" Mom had talked about when she told me about her "falling out" with Hope Grodie? Perhaps the fighting had continued later over the phone lines. It seemed plausible to me—but paranoid to the doctors.

Admittedly, stating that her neighbor "got mad about it and was going to kill me and my husband for saying it" seems pretty exaggerated. But don't we use that expression all the time when we don't mean it? More often than not, when we say something like 'I could've killed him,' it's not a confession of homicidal tendencies, it's simply a measure of the degree of anger that was present at the time.

I was not trying to find a defense for Bertha, I was simply trying to read the record objectively.

Drs. Tate and Hoctor thought my great-grandmother was paranoid because she believed her neighbors were against her. Dr. Hanks did not seem to draw the same conclusion. In his evaluation of her, he noted:

> Says everyone treats her well. Says it was not right that she was sent here and thinks it is not best for her. Says a couple of her neighbors had it in for her is the reason she was brought here. Says companions and friends treated her alright. No one ever followed her or watched her, dectectives [sic] never watched her, no one ever tried to poison her, committed no crimes, and thinks her sins are pardonable. Does not hear strange voices.

In cases of classic, psychotic episodes of paranoia, those affected almost invariably complain of conspiracies against them, of not being able to trust anyone, of being watched or stalked. Bertha did not seem to exhibit any of these irrational fears, especially when she stated that "everyone treats her well." She believed that her neighbors—not everyone else in the world—had it in for her. Maybe there was some validity there. Maybe not.

Of further interest was her conversation with the doctors regarding the deaths of the Schamel brothers:

Q. "Wasn't there two children died that you was suppose [sic] to have given arsenic too [sic]?"

A. "Yes."

Q. "Why did they think you gave them arsenic?"

A. "Because the children were at my house when they died."

Q. "How come them to be there?"

A. "The children's mother died and the father brought them to [my] house."

Q. "How long was it after the first child died until the other one died?"

A. "Six weeks."

Q. "Did you want to keep the children?"

A. "No but I didn't want to say no."

Q. "How long were the children there until they taken sick?"

A. "They brought one of them there sick."

Q. "Was the father there at your house when the children died?"

A. "Yes he stayed there all the time the children were sick."

The following statement, without quotation marks, interrupts the lines of question and answer:

States that the doctor was a dope and whiskey fiend.

The questioning continues:

Q. "Was this the physician that doctored most of the people in the town?"

A. "Yes."

Q. "Did you ever suggest that this man was not a fit person to doctor?"

A. "Yes. The government got after him about it."

Q. "Did you suggest to any one that he might give the patients the wrong medicine?"

A. "Yes. He was drunk too when he came to see the children."

Was there anything to substantiate her claim that Dr. Hemker had a substance abuse problem? Or was Bertha simply trying to shift the blame for the poisoning deaths onto someone else? There were more questions raised by her responses than answers offered.

As I sat at my desk and the soft autumn twilight began to fall outside, I read the interview over and over. Whether she was telling them lies or telling them facts, I could not determine. But one thing seemed clear to me; these did not sound like the irrational ravings of a psychotic.

Finally, I set the interview aside and looked through the remainder of her file. Each time there had been any interaction between Bertha and the hospital staff, a line was added to her file and the event duly noted and dated. In the beginning, the span of time between the entries amounts to weeks or months:

December 18, 1928.

Admitted on above date from Franklin County.

January 8, 1929.

Transferred to Hospital on above date.

January 31, 1929.

Transferred from Hospital to Rec. West.

May 11, 1929.

Has had severe attack of pneumonia following flu since coming to the hospital but made a nice recovery.

December 26, 1929.
Continues to be good worker and nice quiet patient.

July 24, 1930.
No change.

As time went on, though, the gap between entries became years; the next line after the cryptic "No change" of July 1930 was dated March 19, 1933. As the years progressed, the amount of information diminished as well, a bare minimum of words used to note the few significant events—tooth extractions, bouts with pneumonia—of her otherwise uneventful life. By the last page, even the date itself becomes a more efficient numeral instead of a word:

9-30-49: Transferred to Hospital

10-1-49: Transferred to Annex 2

8-10-51: Transferred to Hospital

8-20-51: Patient died this date at 2:45p.m.

I counted forty-five lines, representing the last twenty-three years of my great-grandmother's life. There was no mention of any psychiatric evaluation or treatment after the first year.

It seemed incredibly stark and lonely, which made me achingly sad—even though I knew that Bertha's life was not entirely without the warmth and affection of her family members. On a regular basis, at least in the first years, Gene made the seventy-mile trip, first from Catawissa, then from Eureka where he later moved, down to Farmington to see her. Driving along the old roads and bridges in his Essex, it would have taken him several hours to get there, then several hours to return home after his visit. The arduous nature of the journey is undoubtedly why, after a time, the administrators at Farmington began allowing Bertha to leave the hospital on weekend furloughs to spend time with Gene.

My mother reminded me of this when I called her to let her know, at long last, when and how her grandmother had died. I summarized for her the information I'd received from the Mental Health Center.

"Gene used to drive down and take her home with him on the weekends, then take her back a few days later." She had learned this from Jim Gifford, their son. "Gene always loved her, always insisted she was innocent."

There are times, though, when love isn't able to triumph over all the adversities of life. After several years, Gene's visits dwindled, then stopped. He had found companionship with another woman.

But Bertha would have one more visitor before contact with her family members ceased altogether.

After her grandmother's arrest, my mother had returned to Detroit, where her daily activities in the bustling city of the late 1920's had revolved around trying to get good grades at school and dodging the shady characters who seemed drawn like sharks to her mother's boarding house. In an attempt to escape her somewhat chaotic and decidedly dangerous home life, my mother married at the age of fifteen—a marriage that didn't last and left her divorced at the age of eighteen. By that time, she was comfortable with living on her own, making decisions for herself, and she had that fierce—and sometimes defiant—independence of her grandmother and mother. Making her living as a nightclub singer (and, at times, a "taxi dancer"), Ernestine "Pat" West began to travel the country, never staying in any one place too long, just rambling, letting her sense of wanderlust and the direction of the highway choose a path for her. It was during this time that she decided to find her grandmother.

She doesn't remember what she was thinking on the long drive down to Farmington, her only desire was to see Bertha again. For a decade since the trial, family members—when she could get them to talk at all about the subject—had dismissed the discussion by reiterating that her grandmother was "not right in the head," and would not elaborate beyond that. The young Ernestine had no idea what she would find at this institution which purportedly housed patients ranging from the criminally insane to those suffering from syphilitic dementia. When she arrived, she asked to see Bertha Gifford. She was taken to a large common room and asked to wait. Moments later, her grandmother walked in. Their last meeting had been in the jail in Union when Bertha was awaiting trial for murder and my mother had been ten years old.

"Do you know who I am?" the now twenty-year-old woman asked.

"Of course I know who you are," Bertha answered. "You're Ernestine." With that, the two sat down and had a visit which my mother described to me as "pleasant."

"But what did you talk about?" I asked. The conversation spun exclusively around how Bertha was "getting along." She said she was comfortable, that they treated her well, that she pretty much had the run of the place. My mother remained with her for about an hour.

"She looked good," Mom said. Bertha showed her granddaughter around the hospital and the grounds. And then their visit was over. Ernestine said good-by, got back in her car and drove away. She never visited or contacted her grandmother again, nor did anyone else in the family—including and especially her son Jim, who believed fully in her guilt and had never forgiven her for what she had done. Gene had been the sole champion of her innocence, throughout his life refusing to believe that she was capable of intentionally harming anyone.

After that last visit by my mother, the family had simply tried to forget about her. It seems cruel, but it was a different era then, with so many family issues that weren't talked about, so many secrets kept.

By far the most evocative experience I had when I received the information from the Mental Health Center occurred when I had first opened the letter. The stack of photocopies had been folded in thirds lengthwise, like any business letter. When I unfolded them, the page on top included the copy of a photograph that had been taken of Bertha when she had arrived at the State Hospital. I stared, disbelieving. It was like looking into the face of my mother. The features were exactly the same. Not only their likeness but something else was familiar as well, though I couldn't place it for a long time. Then I realized what I had recognized. I dug through my file and pulled out the pictures I had taken in Missouri. Flipping through them quickly, I found it: The photo I had taken of my mother sitting on the judge's bench in the courtroom. I held the two pictures side by side. Beyond the similarity of heritage, it was an uncanny resemblance in terms of posture and overall appearance—right down to the short, straight hairstyles and nearly identical eyeglasses they wore.

At that moment, something changed inside of me. A tiny door clicked open in my heart and the chamber there became flooded with feelings of familial attachment, of kinship, of affinity by affiliation. She had died before I was born, but she was no longer just a strange persona to be studied. She had given birth to my grandmother who had given birth to my mother who had given birth to me, just as I had given birth to my daughter and she, to hers. For better or for worse, we shared blood and DNA. I saw in her face the same resilient determination I've seen in my mother's face…and that others have seen in mine.

Chapter Fifteen
The Mad Woman in the Asylum

What I was left with, after my attempts to find closure for my mother, amounted to a folder filled with newspaper clippings, some photos of a house and a barn and a courtroom, and copies of a medical file that compressed a very complex woman's life into doctor's visits and dental treatments. At best, my grandiose notion of a quest to learn the truth had created quite an interesting conversation piece. At worst, it had uncovered facts that, as far as my mother was concerned, were probably better off left buried.

Fall turned into winter, winter to spring and then it was blessed summer again and my life careened away from the mad woman in the asylum. I was still recovering from my divorce and struggling, as I suspect many of us do in middle age, to make sense out of what my life had become compared with how I had envisioned it years ago. I was supposed to be a writer. I had planned my life, even my career as a teacher with long summers off, to focus around the creative expression which gave my life meaning and my heart some sense of consolation in a world I had found to be incredibly harsh. In all my life, writing has been the one beacon to guide me back to safe ground when I felt I was being carried me off into darkness and the depths of grief. And yet, even though I had managed to publish a book on prepared childbirth and a few magazine articles over the years, the gods in this odyssey of adulthood seemed to conspire incessantly to sweep me ever further from living the life of quiet introspection I needed to produce articulate prose.

I will always contend that raising four children is not difficult; raising four adolescents as a single parent, and doing it well, is impossible. After my divorce, I tried as best I could to be mother, father, provider, chaperone, chauffeur, confidant, friend and sole disciplinarian. I struggled financially, struggled emotionally, struggled with the question of how I had come to be on this strange path so far from the direction I had intended. My greatest struggle, of course, was in trying to push away the long, cold fingers of depression that I felt closing over my face at night, threatening to smother me in darkness. And now that I knew about my great-grandmother, I thought of her in these times. I thought of how my mother had worried that whatever twisted trait it was which compelled her to do those things she did would be the legacy passed down to subsequent generations. I wrote in a journal at the time:

"I feel as if I am holding onto sanity by a gossamer thread, that somehow it is a conscious choice I make day by day, night by night, not to let go, though it requires every ounce of my strength to hang on, and it is only for the love of my children that I do so. It would seem so easy to simply release my hold on sanity and to fall freely into the depth of this depression that now drags at me. What madness would I find there? And is it inevitable that I will someday discover it?"

Then in the midst of it all, I had an idea, one sleepless night, for a novel. A character came to mind and then that character's plight and then that character's salvation and it all came so fast that I had to get up out of bed and type as fast as my fingers could hit the keyboard to get it all down, an entire outline in one shot. Now I had a sense of purpose and I began to work passionately on the writing of it whenever I could.

Shortly thereafter, my oldest daughter divorced after a brief marriage and came back home to live with me—bringing her two-year-old son with her. Ben's birth had been a joyful event in our family. His presence brought us all together—my daughters and my sons— in a way we had not been since our household had been fragmented by divorce. We all doted on him. I told my daughter I would support her while she went back to school and earned her degree. I was still making a teacher's salary, so I took a second job teaching college classes at night. At the high school, I was asked to teach Journalism and advise the school newspaper so I took that on as well because it paid an extra stipend and it involved writing. The following year, I was asked to do the yearbook as well, and I accepted the position.

There have been those who have called me a "workaholic." (The mutated word by itself makes me cringe.) My long hours had nothing to do with being addicted to work. I was simply trying to put food on the table for everyone and pay the mortgage.

At some point during those years, I took a third job—but this one didn't require me to leave the house. I was asked to write a weekly column for a small local newspaper group. I took it, because it forced me to write something every week, whether I thought I had the time or not, and it gave me a reason to go in my room and close the door with the excuse that I had to get my column finished before deadline. Work on my novel ceased; the chapters were put neatly away in a manila file folder in a drawer. At times I would long to take them out, try to pick up the thread where I had left it and begin again to embroider the grand design that had appeared in my mind so long ago. But there was never, ever time for such work, and I carried with me a constant, quiet grief because of it.

Despite the fact that I was only writing newspaper columns and not the great American novel, I maintained my involvement in a writers group which had started up the same year Mom and I had gone to Missouri. I did so primarily to force myself to venture out into the world of adults twice a month. Had I not, I'm convinced that the loneliness and isolation I had felt for most of my life would have simply overwhelmed me.

So it was on a balmy spring evening that Joyce Spizer, author of detective novels and nonfiction books in the "True Crime" genre, came to speak to our group about writing and marketing. I had met

Joyce once before and liked her immediately. She is funny, personable, and a sharp business woman.

I told her, as she was setting up for the informal talk she would present to us, that my great-grandmother was a serial killer. I had never used the term to characterize Bertha before, but I'd been looking at the cover of one of Joyce's books and I realized that a contemporary audience would classify her in that way.

Joyce asked me how many people she had killed.

"Eighteen, possibly," I said.

"When?"

"She was arrested in 1928."

"Are you writing the book?"

"No."

"Are you kidding? Why not?"

I didn't know. Over the years, the subject had come up from time to time. People were always fascinated with the story. Many times I had heard, "You should write a book about it." I hadn't ever considered it because I didn't want to bring pain or embarrassment to my mother. When we'd taken our trip to Missouri, I'd been able to record very little of our trip in my journal; every time Mom noticed me with a notebook and pen she'd ask, "You're going to write about this, aren't you?" in a tone which made it clear that she disapproved. Beyond my mother's feelings, I'd been reluctant to dwell on a subject so dark at a time when I was struggling to find any illumination at all in my life. I told Joyce as much. She understood.

"But if you ever decide to," she told me, "let me know." She promised to help me when it came time to try to market the book and I knew she would but I didn't think I could write it without my mother's blessing. I thought about it for days. Finally, I took a drive up to see her. We talked about news for awhile. Then I told her.

"I've been thinking about writing a book about your grandmother." There was a long pause as she sat very still and stared at me.

"Well, I think you should," she said. "I was wondering when you were going to get around to it."

My mother's capacity to reverse herself is worthy of Emerson's great adage, "a foolish consistency is the hobgoblin of little minds."

I waited for the summer, for the long blocks of time when school would be out and I could work consistently on the research and writing. In the meantime I pulled out my file on Bertha Gifford, blew the dust off, and began to read again the pages and pages of newspaper stories.

Initially what I found, in re-reading all those articles from the *St. Louis Post-Dispatch*, was very poor journalism. By the time I began serious work on the book, I had taught journalism for six years and had overseen the production of sixty student newspapers. I had been writing for a newspaper for three years, and had also published in other local papers, including the *Los Angeles Times*. Mostly, though, it has been the constant reading, proofing and grading of student journalistic work that has helped me fine tune my appreciation for that particular style of writing; I know what constitutes good journalism, and I definitely know what is bad.

Of course, I had to consider the *Post-Dispatch* pieces in the context of the era in which they were written. From its infancy, the newspaper business, not only in America but abroad, has had as its own tainted legacy the tendency to exaggerate and sensationalize. It has only been in the last several decades that newspapers have begun to collectively sharpen their image, to try to sell papers using truth in their headlines instead of blood. (I am alluding to the old journalistic maxim "If it bleeds, it leads.")

It was especially the case during the "Roaring '20's" that newspapers were catering to the public's demand for as much scintillating gossip as could be splashed across a front page. Like the radical change in fashion, this was a response to the stoic, tight-lipped Victorian Age in which discretion was synonymous with class. By the 1920's, everyone wanted to know everyone else's business. (It is reminiscent, I think, of the voyeuristic "reality" TV shows currently popular.) Back then, a good reporter was always snooping for a juicy scandal, and when found, it would be reported in serial form, with multiple installments and colorful hyperbole.

I came back to the articles about Bertha with a different perspective. When I had first read them, eight years before, I had been trying to discover only what she was guilty of, so, of course, that is what I found, sitting in the library in Frontenac on that very first day we had arrived in Missouri. I found a "poisoner" who had "confessed" to giving arsenic to people who had died, and I found the number of people to be far more than what my mother had thought—the newspaper said seventeen, eighteen if we wanted to give credence to the suspicion that she had murdered her first husband. I had also found that, just like Mom had said, she was "insane" and had been locked up with others like her so that she wouldn't be able to perpetrate her heinous crimes on anyone else.

When I read back through the *Post-Dispatch* stories a second time, and a third and a fourth and a fifth, I read back through them not as the great-granddaughter who is looking with trepidation at her genetic origins but rather as the writer, the journalist, who must maintain objectivity in order to tell the truth as purely as possible. In this way, I saw things that I had not seen before.

One of the first things I noticed, and questioned, was the statement Bertha gave to Chief McDonnell on the day she was arrested. The first *Post-Dispatch* article I had found all those years ago, with its huge, bold headline, declared, "Woman Confesses Giving Poison to Three Persons Who Died in Her Home." The story went on to detail her "confession" to Chief McDonnell. In contrast, the *New York Times'* presentation of the same story stated that "Mrs. Gifford was taken to the Franklin County Jail at Union where it was reported she signed a statement that she herself had frequently taken a poison as medicine and had given it to the five persons along with medicine left by doctors." A "statement" is not necessarily equal to a "confession."

I went back and reviewed that section of the *Post-Dispatch* article once more. Several things suddenly became clear.

The first was this: It seems doubtful that Bertha left the farmhouse that fateful day in August of 1928 with the understanding that by the end of the day she would be in the Franklin County jail. If we consider her strong, belligerent personality under other circumstances, it seems out of character for her to compliantly powder her face, don a nice hat, and quietly leave her husband and children to be carted off to jail, as my mother so vividly recalled it and as the newspaper had later verified. In fact, in Chief McDonnell's later testimony to the court, he stated that Bertha had been willing to talk to him about the case but that she "didn't want to be locked up in the jail." He reassured her by telling her, "We never locked up a woman in my district," then proceeded—with her cooperation—to question her about what some of her neighbors were saying, that a child, Beulah Pounds, had died in her home. She insisted that the child had gotten sick from something she'd eaten, and that she'd never given her any arsenic.

"Well, who did you give it to?" Chief McDonnell had asked her—and she readily told him that when Dr. Hemker had given "medicine" to one of the Schamel boys and it hadn't been effective, she had given him "a little arsenic" to "quiet his pains." She had done the same a month later when the other Schamel boy fell ill, and with Ed Brinley when he had become ill at the farmhouse. She told him that the amount of arsenic she gave Brinley was "not much," and that she sometimes took twice as much herself.

McDonnell summarized the information that Bertha had given him and wrote it into a statement which she read and willingly signed. When I looked at the language of the statement again ("I, Bertha Gifford, hereby state of my own free will, without threat or promise of immunity…."), it became quite apparent, in comparison with Bertha's style of expressing herself and considering her fifth grade education, that it was McDonnell who wrote it. I believe that Bertha, in her naiveté, thought the statement to be nothing more than her telling of the facts as they had happened. Had she thought for one moment that she was being hauled in to the county seat to be thrown in jail, I think there would have been an entirely different outcome on that day—she would, at the least, have protested, if not resisted.

The day after her arrest was the day the *Post-Dispatch* displayed the headline about her "confessing giving poison," and that is when we see Bertha react with anger—and of course, the *Post-Dispatch* reporter was there to immediately file another story describing how she "shed her mask of bravado" and "berated McDonnell because newspapers printed her confession yesterday." From that point forward, the statement, whenever referred to by the press, was characterized as a "confession," and phrases like 'the Missouri farmwife who has confessed to poisoning' were used again and again throughout the stories covering her arrest and trial. (Gene Gifford, of course, represented the lone voice crying out in protest that she had never meant to confess to anything, but no one was listening.)

With this kind of publicity, finding an impartial jury would seem unlikely.

Certainly if Bertha had gone to trial today, the first of many pretrial motions would have been to ask for a change of venue. As it was, the jury that heard the case was selected from friends and neighbors and family members of the Giffords—and of the alleged victims.

In Bertha's case, there were no pretrial motions. And as I began to look back through the *Post-Dispatch* articles which covered the trial, I made another discovery: I had never read them. When we found them, I had quickly scanned the headlines and subtitles, thinking to myself that I would read them thoroughly at a later date. I hadn't done so on our trip. When we came home, I put the file away and never really looked at it again. But now I pulled it out with renewed fascination.

Chapter Sixteen
The Day Ed Brinley Died

With the preponderance of personal testimony that was given at the second Grand Jury hearing, it may seem odd at first consideration that Prosecutor Frank W. Jenny made the decision to try Bertha for the murder of Ed Brinley only. No doubt, though, he had weighed the evidence—and found it lacking. Though folks might point fingers at Mrs. Gifford, no one had actually seen her poison anyone. The fact of the matter is, the only evidence the State had was circumstantial; quite a few people had died in her home, true, but then she was, after all, a volunteer nurse and folks in the community had been bringing her 'patients' for decades. How many sick people were brought to her who ultimately recovered? In addition, the State had failed to establish any motive, which was not a necessary element but one that would have greatly strengthened the prosecution. In the end, Jenny felt that, with Ed's death being the most recent (thus increasing the accuracy of any toxicology examination) and the only one in which family members were clamoring for justice, he would bring Bertha to trial on this one count. If by some chance she was acquitted (despite having already been found guilty in the media and in the court of public opinion), his intention was to then bring her to trial for the deaths of the Schamel brothers.

On the face of it, the Brinley case seemed pretty straightforward. Like many others, Ed Brinley visited the Gifford home, grew sick while there and died shortly thereafter. When his body was exhumed and an autopsy was performed, arsenic was found to be present in his stomach and liver. Furthermore, Prosecuting Attorney Jenny had procured the "poison book" from Powers' Drug Store which clearly showed Bertha's signature on the date of May 16, 1927. She had purchased one ounce of arsenic the day Ed Brinley died.

As clear cut as the case seemed at the outset, however, I came to see as I read through the newspaper clippings that Frank Jenny had a tough time of it since he had to draw on the accounts of neighbors and family members to make his case—none of whom seemed to be able to agree on who did what to whom. At the very least, they did agree on the following facts:

On the evening of May 15, 1927, Ed Brinley showed up at the Giffords', not feeling well. (George Schamel, father of the Schamel brothers, would testify in court that he had known Ed Brinley for forty years, and for all of those years, Ed had been a drunkard. Brinley's age at the time of his death was forty-eight.) Brinley sat with Gene and Bertha for awhile that night in the house, but felt suddenly ill, and when he went outside, he collapsed. Gene Gifford picked up the ailing man, carried him back into the house and made a bed for him in the front room where he slept that night. The next day Ed continued to complain of being sick, though he ate a ham sandwich in the morning and drank some lemonade—followed by some of Gene's home brew—later in the day. His mother and Dr. Hemker had been called. The latter prescribed some medication for the ailing man, and his mother sat with him, talking to him and tending to him. Brinley died later that afternoon. Dr. Hemker, concerned now that so many deaths had occurred with Bertha in charge, consulted with a second doctor before signing a death certificate. After the doctors consulted, a certificate was eventually signed by Hemker. It recorded Edward Brinley's cause of death as "acute gastritis."

Frank Jenny went into the trial claiming that Bertha Gifford was "legally sane." It appears that his intent was to get a straight murder conviction from the jury—the punishment for which was hanging. W. L. Cole, Bertha's attorney, agreed wholeheartedly that his client was sane—and innocent as well. He entered a not guilty plea on her behalf at her arraignment (in her absence, since Bertha felt physically unable to attend).

It seems that both Cole and Jenny presented themselves before the court equally confident, each man prepared to prove his case beyond a doubt.

Chapter Seventeen
No Space in the Aisles

On the first day of her trial, November 19, 1928, my great-grandmother entered the courtroom wearing a dark fox fur collared coat, gray silk stockings and black high-heeled slippers. Her graying hair had been stylishly bobbed. Beneath her coat could be seen the flash of a deep crimson scarf which matched the dark circles of rouge on her cheeks. She had lost a considerable amount of weight and no longer retained her rounded, farmwife appearance. Later in the day, after the lunch break, Bertha's appearance would be altered. When she returned, her cheeks no longer flamed with rouge but had been whitened with powder, reportedly on the advice of her attorney.

On this day, the first business of the court was to voir dire a jury. Circuit Judge Ransom A. Breuer, who would preside over the trial, had summoned to court thirty-eight citizens of Franklin County—all males—and had prevailed upon them to perform their civic duty by participating in jury selection for this trial. (In many states at the time, including Missouri, women had not yet been granted the right to serve on juries.) Thirty of those called had shown up. The men waited patiently to be interviewed by prosecuting attorney Frank Jenny and Mrs. Gifford's attorneys. (W. T. Cole had asked James Booth to assist him in the defense.)

The courtroom was crowded. Bertha's alleged crimes had stretched out over so long a period of time and to so many families in the tiny community in which she lived that there didn't seem to be a single individual in the county whose life had not been affected in some way. The fact that this was a circuit court and Bertha had waited nearly three months for the trial to commence was probably a boon; the humid heat of August during this era before central air conditioning might have proved unbearable.

Bertha was uneasy in the limelight. She sat looking grimly on, her face drawn and lined, the corners of her mouth turned down, as people she knew—and had no doubt tended to when they were sick—were questioned as prospective jurors.

Do you have children?

Are any of those children girls?

Ed Brinley had left behind four children, three of whom were girls—and all of which were considered "orphans," despite the fact that he was survived by a widow who would raise them. The defense would attempt to avoid accepting jurors with large families. Though this was a logical strategy, it must have proved difficult considering the time period and the propensity of farming families to have large numbers of children.

Just behind Bertha sat Gene, dressed this day in a blue suit and sporting an orange and purple striped tie. Despite the weeks of unflattering depictions of Bertha in the press, sentiment toward Gene had remained positive and sympathetic.

The process of jury selection was long and tedious. By afternoon, the farmers who would have had to attend to morning chores had now had the opportunity to get to the courthouse. The correspondent for the *Post-Dispatch* described the scene:

> The afternoon crowd is double the size of the morning crowd. There is no space in the aisles. It is a more representative crowd. Just as many white collar folk as attended the morning session are there, but there are far more men in jumpers. Tall, bronzed men lean against window frames in the white-plastered courtroom holding up infants who from time to time wail. The courtroom has seats for 180.

At least 20 persons are standing. Elderly farm
women, possibly users, before her indictment, of one
of Mrs. Gifford's home compounded potions for
sprains, watch the proceedings self-consciously. A
2-year-old in [the] seventh row yells for a drink of
water.

By 2:30 p.m., a jury had been chosen.

The trial began as soon as the jury had been selected. (This being
circuit court, time was at a premium. Court proceedings began early
and continued far into the afternoon.) After opening statements were
presented, the state still had time before the end of the day to call two
witnesses. The first, Mrs. Henry Grodie, had been a neighbor of the
Giffords for nineteen years. (Here was the name, Grodie. I knew I had
seen it as I'd skimmed the newspaper articles years before. The
woman testifying would have been the future mother-in-law of
Mildred Grodie, whom my mother and I met that morning in Missouri
when we went looking for the farm.)

Mrs. Grodie testified that while Ed Brinley was ill, Bertha had
commented to her, "I hope he don't die in my house." Defense
attorney Booth was quick to point out that this differed from what
Jenny had quoted in his opening statement. The prosecuting attorney
had claimed that Bertha had told Mrs. Grodie, "I hope he don't die
under my roof like the others did."

Despite the fact that she had been called to testify for the State,
Defense Attorney Booth, during cross examination, was able to
extract from Mrs. Grodie the statement that it was Mary Brinley, Ed's
mother, who had given him the lemonade and home brew that seemed
to make him nauseated, not Bertha. This revelation must have had a
strong impact on the jury and everyone in attendance.

The second witness that afternoon was Ludelphia Brinley, Ed's
Brinley's widow. One can only imagine the tension in the courtroom

as the wife of the deceased man took the stand in front of her husband's alleged murderer. The Post-Dispatch reporter described it this way:

> The high point of the afternoon came when Mrs. Ludelphia Brinley, widow of the man Mrs. Gifford is charged with murdering, faced her from the witness chair.
>
> "Is Mrs. Bertha Gifford, the woman you have known for so many years, the defendant seated there at the table?" Prosecuting Attorney Jenny asked.
>
> Mrs. Brinley was obviously under emotional strain. She clasped her hands tightly in her lap and glared at Mrs. Gifford. The latter raised her eyes and the two women exchanged momentary glances. Then Mrs. Gifford, seeming to sink lower in her seat, dropped her eyes. Mrs. Brinley nodded her head vigorously.
>
> "Yes," she said.

Mrs. Brinley testified that, the day after Ed's death, she and Bertha stood outside the house where Ed was laid out. Bertha told her that she knew his mother would be upset by his death, but that she "would really be a heap better off" now that Ed was dead, and that she wouldn't have to worry about him any more.

Booth's cross-examination of Ludelphia clarified why she had not been summoned when Ed fell ill, arriving at the Gifford home only after he had passed away: The Brinleys had separated two years before his death due to his constant "drunkenness." The defense attorney also elicited from her the fact that most of the profits from the butcher shop the Brinleys had once owned had gone to support Ed's drinking, forcing him to finally close the shop and return to farm labor. Certainly this was a tactic used on the part of Booth to both reinforce Ed's compromised health and to decrease the jury's sympathy for his widow.

By the end of the first day in court, Booth had managed to strike a few significant fissures in the seemingly rock solid case against Mrs. Gifford—and to raise the ire of the reporter for the *Post-Dispatch*, who summarized the day's proceedings in this way: "At the opening day of the trial…the failure of more than one State witness to 'bear down' on Mrs. Gifford apparently aided the defense."

Chapter Eighteen
"Don't Let Them Dig up Ed's body"

Though Bertha's defense attorneys had won some battles on the first day of trial, attorneys for the prosecution rallied on the second day. The newspaper account recorded it, in part, as follows:

> The prosecution scored heavily against Mrs. Bertha Gifford today on the second day of her trial for the poison murder of Edward R. Brinley, one-time Pacific (Mo.) butcher who turned farm laborer after taking to drink. Prosecuting Attorney Jenny put on the stand elderly Mrs. Mary Brinley, mother of the man of whose murder Mrs. Gifford is accused and through her testimony offset the gains made yesterday by the defense.
>
> In her seventies, wearing black, the witness drew affectionate nods from the crowded courtroom as she took the witness stand with a distinct show of dignity. She turned her keen eyes full on the tall, soft-spoken Prosecuting Attorney and made replies in a clear, dry voice. She seemed the embodiment of a New England grandaunt painted in the eighties—spare, a little suspicious, but unafraid.

The prosecution's first line of questioning had to do with a conversation Mrs. Brinley had with Bertha some time after Ed had passed away. She claimed that, in a casual conversation ("Oh, we were just talking"), Bertha had said to her, "Don't you let them dig up Ed's body." Apparently their conversation had centered around the neighborhood gossip; people were suspicious of Ed's death and many felt there should have been a post-mortem. Bertha hadn't elaborated on her concern, and it seems fairly obvious that this statement could have been interpreted two ways: Either Mrs. Gifford was afraid of what authorities might find if they exhumed the body, or she was simply encouraging the dead man's mother not to give in to wild tales but rather just to let the dead rest in peace.

Continuing her testimony, Mrs. Brinley explained how Ed had told her, when she arrived at the Gifford home to sit with him while he was sick, that Bertha had given him, throughout the day, two ham sandwiches, a cup of coffee, some lemonade, some "home brew" and medicine that Dr. Hemker had left for him. The elderly woman claimed that it was the lemonade that had caused her son's nausea. In testimony on the previous day, Mrs. Grodie had testified that it was Brinley's mother who had given him the lemonade. The *Post-Dispatch* recorded this exchange:

> "Is it not a fact, Mrs. Brinley," asked [Defense Attorney] Booth, "that you prepared that lemonade yourself?"
>
> "I did no such thing," she replied.

When Booth tried to press her into stating that her son became worse after drinking the lemonade, Mrs. Brinley simply glared at him in her "New England grandaunt" haughtiness. Finally she told him, "He was sick all that day. He was sick before he took the lemonade and after it. He got sick after he ate a sandwich."

Booth then asked her, "How do you know that?" and she replied tersely, "Ed told me so himself."

This hardly seems like a 'score' for the prosecution. If anything, it appears to be conflicting testimony. But the *Post-Dispatch* article continued:

Prosecutor Jenny scored again when he called for William Powers, elderly stooped druggist of Pacific, who is extremely hard of hearing, and who presented evidence to the effect that Mrs. Gifford, on the day that Ed Brinley died, purchased an ounce of arsenic in his drug store at Pacific.

Booth sought to harry the white-mustached druggist, but it was difficult. When the stocky defense lawyer presented his most baffling question, Powers cupped a hand to his ear and said: "How?"

The poison book of Powers' drug store, a small ledger with a bright red cover, in which the signature of Mrs. Bertha Gifford appears opposite the date of May 16, 1927, was passed from hand to hand by jurors.

Dr. Hemker, "neatly dressed and clear spoken," was the next witness brought to the stand by the prosecution. He told of how he'd been summoned to the Gifford home and had found Ed in "acute distress" with stomach pains. He was asked if Ed's consumption of alcohol after the lemonade could have contributed to his gastritis. He admitted that it might but that the effect would not be "toxic."

Next to be called to the stand were the doctors who had performed the examination of Ed Brinley's exhumed body:

Dr. Ralph Thompson of St. Louis, who had conducted inquests for the past 29 years, testified as to the post mortem on Brinley's body. He stated that inflammation existed in the stomach and the kidneys and that he had turned over the viscera to Dr. Harry Bristow, toxicologist and former professor of chemistry at Missouri University, for chemical analysis.

Dr. Thompson said his examination showed no organic disease or infectious malady that would have caused death.

Dr. Bristow testified that he examined chemically the liver and the stomach and he found arsenic in both organs. He said there was at least one grain of arsenic in the liver. Later, on cross examination, Dr. Bristow said that at least five grains of arsenic, in compound form, must have been administered to the murdered man to cause death.

The "climax of the afternoon" (quite accurately characterized by the *Post-Dispatch* reporter) was the battle between Mrs. Gifford's defense attorneys and the prosecution regarding whether or not the "confession" of Mrs. Gifford could be presented to the court as evidence. This was the most critical moment of the trial. Attorney Booth objected to the prosecution's request to admit the statement as evidence, presumably on the grounds that Bertha had never intended it as a confession (which would imply an intent to murder). He asserted that it had simply been a statement of the facts surrounding certain events. In order to try to resolve whether it was the former or the latter, Judge Breuer excused the jury from the courtroom and brought Chief McDonnell to the stand to question him regarding what exactly had transpired when he obtained the statement. It is here that McDonnell presented his intriguing story of the day he arrested Bertha Gifford.

He told how he had received a phone call from Frank Jenny asking him to go out to the Gifford's farm and arrest Bertha Gifford. McDonnell "had some things to do," he said, so he'd brought her to his office in Webster Groves. (Webster Groves is a small community just outside of St. Louis—twenty-five miles or so east of the jail in Union. If his intention that day was to arrest her, it seems odd that he would have taken her such a distance in the opposite direction, nor, we have to believe, would he have told her, "We never locked up a woman in my district.")

McDonnell made Bertha comfortable in a big chair in his office, got her some drinking water and offered her coffee, then left her to tend to whatever compelling business it was that he had to take care of. He returned later to talk to her about the Grand Jury testimony regarding suspicious deaths in her home. She discussed her reasons for giving arsenic to Brinley and the Schamel boys, and then made what can truly be defined as a confession when she told him that she herself would take arsenic.

"I asked her why she took arsenic," the sheriff continued, "and she leaned close to me and said—'I'll tell you why I take it.' She said, 'I take it to make me look young. And when I get puffy under my eyes. And I take it when my heart goes this way.'" McDonnell patted his chest rapidly to demonstrate.

Although her behavior—taking arsenic to make herself stay young looking—might seem outrageous to us today, we have to consider it in the context of the times in which she lived. At that time there were individuals known as "arsenic eaters" who thought they had found a 'fountain of youth' in the heavy metal, and they advocated ingesting it in small amounts on a regular basis in order to keep the skin and tissues youthful. Certainly Bertha knew that arsenic in large amounts is highly poisonous. (So is the active ingredient in Botox injections.) But taking the substance had helped, she believed, to erase some of the signs of age and to alleviate her high blood pressure. In the days following her arrest, in fact, Sheriff Gorg offered some validity to this perspective when he was questioned about Bertha by the *Post-Dispatch* correspondent. Note how the journalist's choice of adjectives ("mystical," "sinister") tints the sheriff's point of view:

> Sheriff Gorg thinks that Mrs. Gifford attributed
> some mystical healing power to arsenic and gave it
> to patients without sinister motive. This point of view

is not shared by either Chief McDonnell or Prosecuting Attorney Jenny.

Bertha's regular use of the toxin becomes even more credible with the realization that *Dr. Hemker gave his patients arsenic—and strychnine*. Although this fact was never explored during the trial (considering, after all, that Mrs. Gifford was a "volunteer nurse"), the good country doctor spoke of it openly with the *Post-Dispatch* reporter:

> In the death of both Schamel children and Brinley, Dr. Hemker says he feared the circumstances [were] so suspicious that he refrained from giving arsenic or strychnine as a heart stimulant because he did not wish to complicate any post-mortem inquiry. He administered digatalin, he said, to stimulate the heart.

In other words, concerned that there might eventually be autopsies performed on these patients whose illnesses seemed sudden and without cause, Dr. Hemker didn't use his standard method of treatment, which was to administer arsenic or strychnine as a heart stimulant, because if arsenic were found in the body later, he wanted to be able to state that it wasn't arsenic *he* had given—even though it would have been perfectly acceptable for him to do so, since he was the physician. And in reality, Dr. Hemker wasn't the one who administered these "medicines," anyway. It was Bertha he supervised as his "volunteer nurse," Bertha with whom he would leave the medicine and the instructions.

During the course of their discussion in Webster Groves, Chief McDonnell had "interrogated" Mrs. Gifford regarding Ed Brinley's insurance and whether she stood to gain from his death or the deaths of the Schamel boys. She insisted she had not profited "a nickel," and he was satisfied that she was telling the truth. McDonnell then prepared the written statement, and Bertha signed it.

After considering the police chief's testimony, Judge Breuer decided that the statement was admissible as evidence.

His decision was crucial to the outcome of the trial. Booth and Cole knew this certainly. The jury was bound to interpret the statement as a confession; they had already read in the paper that it was. With the statement accepted as such, the State could sidestep its burden to prove Bertha's guilt—she had already admitted to her crimes.

The twelve jurors were ushered back into the courtroom and McDonnell testified again in their presence as to the circumstances of the statement. The "confession" was then read into the court record. Finally, another police official from Webster Groves, a man by the name of Ruhe, was called to the stand to testify that he had witnessed Bertha's signing of the document.

Upon the completion of his testimony, the State rested its case.

Immediately Booth was on his feet asking for a directed verdict for an acquittal, claiming that the State had failed to produce substantial evidence to prove murder in the first degree. (In other words, the judge would take the verdict out of the hands of the jury and make it himself.)

Booth's motion for a directed verdict was overruled and court was adjourned. The defense would present its case the following day.

Chapter Nineteen
A Foolish Consistency

My great-grandmother's fate was determined on the third and final day of her trial:

> UNION, Mo., Nov.—21—Counsel for Mrs. Bertha Gifford offered an insanity plea today in an effort to save the middle-aged Catawissa (Mo.) farm woman from the gallows for the poison murder of Edward P. Brinley. After five witnesses, including Gene Gifford, the confessed poisoner's drawling, sad-eyed husband, had gone on the stand to testify that Mrs. Gifford was nervous, morose and excitable, the defense asked for a recess and went into conference with seven physicians.

It had been the strategy all along of attorneys Booth and Cole to base their defense on the fact that every piece of evidence introduced in the trial was circumstantial—every piece except the statement in which Bertha admitted giving arsenic to three people. If that document were construed as a confession, as the prosecution, and certainly the press, had made it out to be, then the jury could—and undoubtedly would—interpret it to be an admission of guilt. Every other piece of evidence was refutable except for that piece of paper. If Bertha had refused to sign it, if she had simply said, "I want to talk to an attorney," as a more system-wary person might do today, the prosecution would have had little more to build a case around other than coincidence and innuendo. This is why Booth had argued so vehemently the day before to disallow the statement. He knew that, without it, the prosecution had nothing to substantiate the charge of murder in the first degree, and Bertha would be acquitted. With it, however—and considering the fact that community sentiment was almost unanimously in opposition to Bertha—the jury would almost of a surety return a verdict of guilty, and a guilty verdict would mean a sentence of death—by hanging. Booth and Cole had to either present an irrefutable defense to prove Bertha's not guilty plea—or they had to change her plea so that, if the jury could not be convinced of her innocence, her life would be spared. Judging by their line of questioning, they had already decided the direction they would take by the time they put Gene Gifford on the stand.

Strangely absent from the courtroom on the previous day, Gene appeared on the morning of the third day of trial as the first witness for the defense. In contrast to her long hours of stoicism during the previous two days, Bertha struggled to contain her emotions when her husband took the stand:

> Mrs. Gifford betrayed emotion for the first time since the opening of the trial Monday, as Gene—who is 10 years her junior and was 22 when she married him in 1906—took his seat in the witness chair. Her knuckles were white as she pressed her clenched hands against her mouth. She listened intently, focusing directly on a witness for the first time.... For the past 10 years, Gifford said, his wife had been restless and frequently she would "just sit down and not have much to say." Frequently he said she would walk the floor for two or three nights, after which she would be "bothered." The floor-walking spells, he said, occurred every three or four weeks.

Gene went on to recount again for the jury the night that Ed Brinley became ill and had to be carried into the house and put to bed. Gene claimed it was he, not Bertha, who had made the ham sandwich for Brinley the next day. Gene had left the house to go to work on the farm after that and, he stated upon cross examination, he was unaware that his wife had also left the house that morning—to go to Pacific where she would buy arsenic.

Four more witnesses for the defense were called to the stand following Gene's testimony to speak in regard to Bertha's state of mind. Each one described her as "nervous" and excitable—including Mrs. Henry Frye, who owned the property that Gene Gifford farmed, though Mrs. Frye also characterized Mrs. Gifford as "a kind-hearted woman."

With this foundation laid, the defense team asked for a recess in order to confer with an entire group of physicians who would testify—some on behalf of the State and others on behalf of the defense—as to Bertha's insanity.

It is interesting to note here that the defense had called in five doctors who would give testimony regarding Bertha's diminished mental capacity—all of whom were local medical doctors, general practitioners who were not psychiatrists. The State had likewise summoned two doctors, both psychiatrists, who had not, at this point, ever spoken with Mrs. Gifford; there had been no need to as long as her attorneys sought a straight not guilty verdict. However, in spite of the fact that they had not had the opportunity to evaluate her themselves, they still participated in the conference which took place between the defense attorneys and the other five doctors. After conferring with these seven physicians, Booth and Cole prepared to take their defense in an entirely new direction.

When court reconvened some long moments later, they made a motion to change Mrs. Gifford's plea of not guilty to not guilty by reason of insanity. The motion was granted, and a succession of doctors was called to the stand. Each testified that Bertha suffered from "dementia praecox."

"Dementia" is basically a generic term in psychiatry used to describe psychotic behaviors ranging anywhere from distorted perceptions of reality to hallucinations. The use of "praecox" (or "precocious") to qualify this type of dementia indicates that the dementia begins in a relatively early stage of life (experts use the age of forty-five as a marker) as opposed to dementia which occurs in the elderly as the result of Alzheimer's disease or some other physiological deterioration. In the past several decades, we have come to know this condition as "schizophrenia," which is again a generic term covering a large range of psychotic behavior.

In Bertha Gifford's case, the medical doctors called by the defense to give testimony at her trial all said the same thing: She had morbid obsessions with death and funerals and that she experienced "thrills" in observing sick people, especially those about to die. Based on their interview with her after the second day of testimony, they offered dementia praecox to the jury as an explanation for her presumed propensity to commit murder.

Despite the fact that the State had rested its case on the previous day, the change in plea gave Frank Jenny the opportunity to bring forth his two final witnesses. One at a time, the psychiatrists from St. Louis, Dr. George A. Jones and Dr. P. J. Farmer, took the stand. Each in turn was read the transcript of the trial testimony regarding Ed Brinley's death and Bertha's struggle with depression and anxiety after having gone through menopause (her "physical crisis in life") ten years before. Each was asked the question, "What is your opinion as to the sanity of the defendant?" Each replied in turn, "She is unquestionably of unsound mind, suffering from chronic paranoia, incurable."

Here again, "paranoia" is a somewhat general term in psychiatry and can mean many things. Today the word is often misused. Basically, being suspicious, fearful or anxious is not enough to constitute paranoia in the psychotic sense. True paranoia involves a deep-seated fear that is unsubstantiated or irrational, and this fear can manifest itself in many ways. Specifically, though, someone who is diagnosed as a paranoid schizophrenic may suffer from delusions or hallucinations or both.

It seems apparent that the prosecution was just as interested as the defense in demonstrating to the jury that Bertha Gifford was insane. Frank Jenny would later tell the *Post-Dispatch* reporter, "The woman is incontestably insane and has been so for years. That is my conviction. In the face of that, I couldn't insist on the death penalty or prison." It appears that Mr. Jenny had the same appreciation for Ralph Waldo Emerson and his disdain for a foolish consistency as my mother has; he was just as convinced at the onset of the trial that Bertha was "legally sane," and went on record as saying that he would seek the death penalty.

All witnesses having been exhausted by both sides, the State again rested its case, as did the defense. The jury, then, withdrew to deliberate.

Initially, I wondered why Booth and Cole did not have Bertha testify in her own defense. If I were a defense attorney, and I was defending a crazy woman—and trying to prove she was crazy so she wouldn't be convicted of murder—why wouldn't I put her on the stand? Let her babble on for awhile, show the jury just how out of touch with reality she really was. But as I read back over the newspaper account of the court proceedings again and again, analyzing the strategies on both sides, and I considered how Bertha's testimony would come across on the stand, I understood. In her interview (or "interrogation") with Chief McDonnell and later with the psychiatrists at Farmington, Bertha was calm, quiet and lucid. She answered questions carefully and in a relatively articulate manner, considering her education and background. She was characteristically abrupt and sometimes brusque, and occasionally there could be perceived the slight edge of anger in her tone, but she seemed entirely coherent. If her attorneys had put her on the stand for questioning, she undoubtedly would have appeared quite sane to the twelve men observing her. In fact, with her demeanor and terse responses, they might easily have seen her as fitting the newspaper's portrayal of a cold, calculating murderer.

It took the jury three hours to bring back its verdict. At the first polling, eleven voted not guilty. A farmer from Franklin County had not been convinced by the medical testimony and felt that Mrs. Gifford should be punished for her crimes. He continued to insist, for three hours, that she was guilty of murder. Finally he acquiesced, and at 10:20p.m. the jury returned to the courtroom and the verdict was announced: Not guilty by reason of insanity.

Judge Breuer immediately declared that she would be remanded to an institution for the criminally insane for the remainder of her life.

Bertha left the courtroom "on the arm of her farmer husband…plainly sunk in an extreme melancholy."

In a section subtitled "Doctors' Guesses," the *Post-Dispatch* reporter offered speculation as to the motive for Bertha's crimes, since the State never established one:

> No one knows the entire history of this woman, once beloved by a countryside for her seeming Samaritanism and later feared as a furtive poisoner. The physicians who talked with Mrs. Gifford all came away with the opinion that she had a sort of Messianic delusion that she was the best judge of life and death for her friends and associates. They suspected that she poisoned the Schamel boys because their mother had died and there was no one to look after them—that she wanted them to join their mother "in Heaven" and believed, through killing them, she was doing good.

> They think that she killed Ed Brinley with an idea that she was benefiting humanity because Ed was a wastrel who did not support his family, his life was

insured, and his widow needed the money. Further examination of the list of 18 persons at whose bedsides Mrs. Gifford was a volunteer nurse and who died suddenly, shows the possibility of this "doing good" twist in Mrs. Gifford's warped mentality....

The world that Bertha Gifford knows is beyond doubt a crazy, morbid world that will never be revealed. When the physicians taxed her with poison murders, tears stood in her eyes, her nostrils dilated, and she said in her quaking voice: "But I wanted to help them. I wanted to do good."

Chapter Twenty
"A Realization of Her Status Before the Law"

Unless you experience it for yourself, you can't fully appreciate the wonder, the beauty, the freedom, the independence that comes when you drive across this country. From where I live in Southern California, you can catch Highway 40 and it will carry you on its smooth gray back through the incredible painted desert of Arizona, past the miraculous red mesas of New Mexico and the sprawling vistas of Texas and bring you gently to the rolling green hills of Oklahoma, then onto the 44 and up through the gorgeously verdant countryside of Missouri. I can't say for certain whether I was enamored of the highway or the idea of returning to the spot where the mysteries had begun. Either way, I found myself traveling, in early July of 2003, back to Pacific, Catawissa and all the places I had discovered on my last trip to Missouri, nearly nine years before.

In reading through the newspaper stories, I had found there were pieces missing, details of facts and features that I needed in order to adequately flesh out the deeds—or misdeeds, as it were—of Bertha Gifford. Really, that was just an excuse. I wanted to go back to where Mom and I had started our search, to make sure we hadn't left any stones unturned. And, after all those years, the farmhouse on Bend Road still called to me. Beyond all that, I needed to get away. It had been a tough year.

When the school year had started the previous fall, I'd taken a job working for a different high school because it was a great opportunity and it was closer to home. Unfortunately, I had to take a cut in pay.

The year prior, I had quit teaching college classes in order to have time to write, but I had to go back to teaching those classes again to make up the income deficit. Spending the day with one hundred eighty teenagers can be fun and it is often rewarding but it is always, always, exhausting. I would teach at the high school all day, then two afternoons a week head straight to the college to teach my classes there, then come home in the evening and try to continue my research. I was tired all the time. And I began to feel as if I were losing in my fight against the vortex of a depression which constantly threatened to overwhelm me.

I battled daily, during that time, against giving in to feelings of despair. What kept me afloat was my driving determination to be an effective teacher, a nurturing mother and a loving, affectionate Nana, but it was with great difficulty that I did so.

By the time the school year ended, I felt relieved to have survived it, and I anticipated time to sleep and time to write. Both came, eventually, in large, healthy amounts.

I spent my days writing and planning my trip and, when the time came, I packed my Dodge pick-up truck with what I would need for two weeks, and then I hit the road. I made it to Missouri in three days because I just couldn't wait to get there. This time I would stay in Pacific, as it was close to all the places I wanted to visit.

Driving ten hours a day for three days gave me a great deal of time to think—which is not usually healthy for a person of my temperament. In this case, though, it gave me time to review my feelings on Bertha's trial and what had happened there.

When I teach Shakespeare's *Romeo and Juliet* to high school freshmen, they invariably ask the question, "Why didn't Romeo and Juliet just run away together?" as if the star-crossed lovers could have fled Verona on horseback to some tiny Italian hamlet where no one would know them and where Romeo could take a job at a tortellini factory to make ends meet while Juliet stayed at home to care for the baby they would most assuredly have had in the first year. I try to teach my students that we have to accept literature and history in the context of its setting. In the case of my great-grandmother, I was finding it hard to follow my own caveat.

Several things made me angry. One was that she was not tried by a jury of her peers because the jury was made up entirely of men, which might have made a tremendous difference to me were it not for the fact that everyone seemed to suddenly think Bertha was definitely crazy after her husband got on the stand and testified that she had been different ever since she went through menopause. Gene said that she was "morose" and that she had trouble sleeping. We know now that these are chemical and physiological responses to a natural body change which comes with age. That doesn't mean she was crazy. Tense, agitated, irritable, prone to mood swings, perhaps. But criminally insane? Homicidal? And if we believe the stories of those who gave testimony before the grand jury, the fact of her passing the 'crisis of her life' ten years before had nothing to do with her crimes, since her alleged poisonings began as far back as 1912, possibly even 1906 if we want to suspect that she poisoned her first husband, Henry Graham. No, the testimony that emerged from the emotionally devastated Gene Gifford, who had insisted all along that his wife was absolutely innocent but now talked sadly of her altered state of mind, was obviously a ploy by her attorneys to persuade the jury not to hang her. The same is true of the psychiatrists' testimony, which I suppose evoked more anger in me than anything else. They never even spoke to her. They showed up and took the stand, each in his turn, and were read the transcript from the previous two days of testimony and were asked to make a judgment based on that alone and they did. Both of them said that she was incurably insane. Those men who controlled her fate—the judge, the jury, the attorneys on both sides had found the least offensive way to get rid of her by sending her off to Farmington. They knew, I'm sure, that once she was institutionalized she would never return to the community. Did she give arsenic to Ed Brinley and the Schamel boys? Yes, unequivocally. She admitted she did. Did she do it so that they would die horrible, painful deaths? I was simply not convinced of that. Those "delusions" the psychiatrists brought up in order to explain her motivation for murder—How did they substantiate them? They never interviewed or evaluated Bertha. And that degree of psychosis was not found by the psychiatrists who evaluated her at the state hospital. In fact, the psychiatrist specifically assigned to her case had found no psychosis at all.

I do realize that, had not these men conferred and agreed together regarding the outcome they wanted for the trial, my great-grandmother would have been hanged. There is no doubt that she would have been found guilty. That's the way things were back then. It didn't make it any easier to accept the fact that she had spent nearly a third of her life isolated from her family and loved ones.

I thought of all this as my truck carried me over the miles. And I thought of something I had learned from Ray Bradbury years ago about being a writer, and the power to change history. 'If you don't like the way Hemingway died, write a story with a time machine and resurrect him' (which is, indeed, what Bradbury did). But the power to manipulate our medium according to our creative imagination comes only with the writing of fiction. This strange tale about my great-grandmother revolved around people who had really lived, people who had really died, and there was no time machine to bring them back, or to go to them and intervene, as much as I would have liked to. Whatever happened had happened many years ago, though it could have happened yesterday and it wouldn't have mattered any more or any less; what was done was done. And the saddest aspect of it all was that the ultimate truth had died when Bertha Gifford died. She was the only person who knew for sure whether or not she had ever meant to hurt anyone.

When I finally arrived in Pacific after three days of being alone on the road with all those unanswerable questions swirling in my head, the youthful smiles of Chris and Amanda, the night clerks at the Holiday

Inn where I stayed, were a warm and welcome sight. They cheerfully checked me into my room, and I settled in with all my notes and writing paraphernalia. For some reason, it almost felt like coming home.

Because I had so recently spent weeks reading and analyzing Bertha's trial, I wanted to go to the courthouse again, to make sure my memory had served me well in describing it after all these years. I also wanted to double-check with the circuit court clerk regarding whether or not there were transcripts of the trial. (I just couldn't believe a trial of that import would not have been documented other than the judgment. Alas, it was not. "Nope, sorry," the clerk told me. "Transcripts were only kept if an appeal was filed. And even if we had kept them, they would have been destroyed years ago.") But my most important mission at the courthouse on my first morning back in Missouri was to try to find out, once again, who owned the farm on Bend Road.

Little had changed in downtown Union. I found the courthouse easily and parked the truck across the street. Before going in, I snapped a few pictures, and as I did so I noticed a small newspaper office for the *Missourian Tribune*. I went inside and asked the receptionist if the Tribune had been in existence in 1928.

"You know, I don't know," she said. "I've only been with the paper a short while. You could ask over at the library. They've got old copies of the paper on microfilm."

I thanked her and strolled back across the street to the courthouse. Once inside, I went straight to the county recorder's office, handed the clerk a slip of paper with the address of the farmhouse, and waited while she disappeared into a back room for not longer than two minutes. She returned, holding a piece of microfiche in her hand.

"The readers are in this other room," she said, directing me across the hall. It was all, of course, an elaborate déjà vu; Mom and I had gone through the exact same motions. *Almost* the exact same motions. When the transparency was fitted under the lens and projected onto the monitor, I saw everything I had seen before, with one exception.

There was the Fiedler name and their street address "in town"—but not the town we had thought. Nine years before, when Mom had quickly scribbled down the address, she had failed to record the city. The Fiedlers did not live in St. Louis or Pacific or Catawissa, all cities I had addressed letters to over the years, hoping to find them. The Fiedlers lived in Bridgeton. I'd never even heard of it.

"That's why," I said aloud.

"Pardon?" I realized the patient clerk was waiting for me to get whatever information I needed. I added "Bridgeton" to the same piece of motel stationery we'd used nine years before, thanked her, then went out to roam the courthouse for an hour.

I walked the halls and peeked into rooms for so long, in fact, that a nice gentleman approached me to ask if I could be helped. I'm sure the clerks were beginning to worry about me. I assured him that I was fine, just kind of sight-seeing, and he seemed satisfied. There was a deputy stationed in the lobby and I asked him if he knew where the jail might have been in 1928. I'd read so much about Bertha's stay there, I wanted to see it. He told me the location of the current jail, but it had been built in recent years. He didn't know where the jail might have been in '28.

Unlike the last time I'd been there, court was in session, so I wasn't able to go into the courtroom. During a short recess, I peeked through the window. The room had not changed. Once again I imagined Bertha sitting at the defense table, her attorneys next to her, Gene behind her in his orange and purple striped tie. What was going through her mind in those dramatic days of the trial? Could she ever have expected things would turn out as they did?

I was still pondering her state of mind as I left the courthouse and, returning to my truck, remembered that I wanted to check out the Union library to see if there were copies of the *Missourian Tribune* on microfilm. There were. But the newspaper in 1928 was called the *Republican Tribune* (lest there be any confusion as to where the paper stood politically).

The paper was—and still is—distributed twice weekly, on Tuesdays and Fridays (now as the *Union Missourian*). I found the issues I needed in a matter of several minutes. There was no byline given on the stories and the newspaper is quite small, so it's probably safe to assume that the same person wrote and edited everything that went into it.

I had learned at least one thing from my experience with researching the material on Bertha Gifford: Never skim. (I am convinced that I now have what it takes to be a successful prospector. Even if there were very little chance of me finding any gold, I know I would have the patience to keep swirling the sand around in the pan, endlessly searching.) There was a story on Bertha's arrest in August, then another very short article of one hundred words or so announcing that her trial would probably be in November, and a third with a summary of the trial and the verdict. After I had made photocopies of all three, I sat in the library and carefully read them over. The majority of the first one was comprised of material from the *Post-Dispatch* which the larger paper had given the *Tribune* permission to reprint. There was one brief paragraph, however, that caught my eye:

Mrs. Gifford is being held in the Franklin County jail without bond. Since Saturday she has not been in a conversational mood, but seems to have suffered a realization of her status before the law.

Was I reading between the lines? Or did the reporter seem to corroborate my feeling that Bertha never expected the scales of justice to be so heavily weighted in her disfavor? I set those thoughts aside and went on to the article which chronicled the trial. It provided a concise summary, in two columns, of what had taken place in the courtroom, and it did so with refreshingly straight, objective reporting—until the last paragraph:

The verdict of the jury means that Bertha Gifford will be confined in some asylum for the insane during

> the period of her insanity and which may be the time
> of her natural life. Bertha Gifford is a woman of some
> 52 years of age, and her insanity would not be readily
> detected by persons not skilled in this kind of work.
> She is able to do all kinds of house work, is not violent,
> and the only thing that she did that was wrong was to
> wait on people and put a little arsenic into the doctor's
> medicine with the hope that it would help the patients.

With the exception of Gene Gifford, this was the first voice I'd heard that sounded sympathetic toward my great-grandmother, and I appreciated the writer's stand on her behalf. At the time the newspaper was published, it probably didn't make him a popular man.

I made one more discovery within the lines of the newspaper piece that seemed trivial at the time, but for some reason I decided to jot it down. While Bertha had awaited trial, authorities finally ordered the long-awaited autopsy on the bodies of Ed Brinley and the Schamel brothers. Tucked in neatly at the end of the article was a line noting that Ed Brinley's body had been exhumed from Brush Creek Cemetery.

Before I left the library, I stopped at the desk and asked the two librarians there if either knew where a jail might have been in Union in 1928. Both looked puzzled and said they didn't know, though they, like the deputy, told me about the "new" jail.

If you drive east on Highway 44 from Union there is a turn-off for Robertsville that will lead you to Catawissa if you have a good sense of direction and you know where to catch the right highway. Or it will just get you lost, driving up and down miles and miles of country roads past farms and fences, looking for a way out. I had left Union early in the afternoon and decided to try to find the farmhouse on Bend Road before heading back to the motel. Since I hadn't planned to go, I hadn't brought my maps. I thought I remembered how to get there—and, as it turns out, I almost did. But one wrong turn had gotten me hopelessly lost. I kept driving up and down long, rolling country roads, past farm after farm, trying to find anything that looked familiar or at least a road that intersected that I might remember from the map. It was a hot day—93 degrees and humid. I hadn't eaten since the bagel and bowl of cornflakes I'd had for an early breakfast. I was hungry, sticky, and had intended to spend the afternoon writing. Finally I gave up searching for the farmhouse and, using the compass in my truck, headed due north, the direction of the main highway. After several miles, I emerged from the deeply wooded country that lines the Meramec River, relieved to have found the frontage road which runs parallel to the highway. I was three short miles from the hotel. But all thoughts of finally getting a meal and a shower dissipated as I sat at the intersection and gazed in amazement across the road. Directly in front of me was an arched wrought iron gateway. Beyond it, pale tombstones dotted an acre or so of deep green hills. The Dodge idled in a deep throaty rhythm as I sat with my window down, staring at the sign which read "Brush Creek Cemetery."

How had I come exactly and precisely to this place after reading about it for the first time just hours ago? I felt strongly that in some way or for some reason I was supposed to be here, and just as strongly I knew that I could not leave this place until I had sought out the grave of Edward P. Brinley.

Chapter Twenty-One
"It Could've Happened Yesterday"

I started in the northeast corner of the cemetery, walking slowly through the grass, reading the names on the headstones, thinking about all the things that had brought me to this quiet place two thousand miles from home to wander through a graveyard looking for the headstone of a man who should have at least lived long enough to raise his children...and perhaps have the chance to redeem himself. Ghosts, I thought. Ghosts had brought me here. I was really just trying to connect somehow with those who were long dead, for they were the ones with the answers.

Nearly an hour had passed before I'd made my way carefully up and down every row. I felt faint from the heat and from hunger, and I still hadn't found Ed's grave. Maybe the newspaper had been inaccurate. Maybe his family had decided to move his grave after the autopsy. I thought I'd searched every section. But as it always seems to go in stories like these, as I turned to leave, I noticed a small knoll, walked to the top of it, and from there could see a far corner of the cemetery I hadn't seen previously. I could see the headstone from where I was standing—"Brinley." Seventy-five years had not blurred the polished granite engraving. By the time I walked the thirty yards to where the Brinley family plot was located, I was crying.

Ed Brinley is buried in a row with five of his seven children. His mother, Mary, is buried close by. Off to the side a tall beautiful headstone marks the grave of Ludelphia Brinley, the shy, nervous woman who would not stop pressing for an investigation into the death of her husband.

I can't explain why I sat amid the markers and wept. In order for me to take you to the place of grief and loss that I was experiencing, I'd have to tell you far too much about a childhood spent in isolation, about what it means for a little girl to grow up without a father and then to lose a husband because he simply walks away. More painful, though, was watching my own children grow up without a father; my girls had no Daddy to tell them they were beautiful, the boys had to settle for me alone in the stands at basketball games and track meets. All of this grief was present as I sat among the dead, but I don't think I cried for myself. I suppose I cried not only for Ed Brinley's children, but for all the people whose lives had been irreparably damaged by the actions of my great-grandmother—whether she ever intended harm or not.

Later I would tell my best friend Laura on the phone, "I kept trying to say 'I'm sorry,' but I was crying too hard…which is pointless, I suppose; it happened seventy-five years ago."

"And it could've happened yesterday," she replied, "because they're all dead—there is no time."

And when she said it, I knew that was exactly how I'd felt.

When I finally returned to the Holiday Inn that day, I was emotionally weary. I missed my kids but when I tried to call home, there was no answer. I sat on the bed and listened to the sound of my own voice on my answering machine, then hung up. My eye fell on the phone book. I pulled it off of the nightstand, flopped it open on the bed, and turned to the F's. Fiedler. This time there were twenty-nine of them. But "Robert A." was the only Robert A.—except that it was no longer Robert A. and Claire. Robert Fiedler had a new wife, it seemed. What had happened? A death? A divorce? I suddenly felt like I was prying into his personal life. And just as suddenly ignored all those feelings and picked up the phone and dialed.

"Hello?" a man's voice answered.

"Mr. Fiedler?" I asked, now wondering what I would say if it were really him.

"Yes?" he said. I took a huge breath.

"You don't know me," I told him, "but I've been looking for you for nine years."

"Nine years!" he said, chuckling, "Well, what for?" I liked him right away. I asked him if he still owned the farm on Bend Road. He did. I asked if he knew the history of the house.

"Well, what history would that be?"

"My great-grandmother lived in that house at one time," I said. "She was accused of poisoning some people...."

"Yes, I know quite a bit about that," he said. "My wife was related to one of the people that was poisoned."

"What was your wife's maiden name?" I asked.

"Pounds."

"So her ancestor would have been Sherman Pounds."

"You got it."

He told me that Claire had passed away seven years before—two years after Mom and I had been here the first time. Claire had learned much of the history of the house and the stories about Bertha from her family. Sherman Pounds was Claire's grandfather. After Bertha's trial, Gene moved out of the farmhouse and away from the area. He had been leasing the property from the Frye family. (Mrs. Frye, the Giffords' landlord, had been the only character witness in Bertha's trial to characterize her in a positive way, describing her as "kind hearted.") The Fryes sold the farm to Claire's parents in 1929 and Bob and Claire had eventually purchased it from them.

Though Claire had been the historian in the family, Bob knew a great deal about the story of Bertha Gifford and the various family members whose lives had been affected. We talked for a half hour or so, then he said:

"Well, my wife and I will be going out to the farmhouse tomorrow. Would you like to come out and see the place?" I was thrilled at the invitation, and for a second I wished my mother was there to see the house, to walk around in it and stir up all her good memories of living there. But I knew that she would still find it awkward. I made arrangements to meet with Mr. Fiedler at eleven o'clock the next day. When I slept that night, I dreamt of walking through the farmhouse.

Chapter Twenty-Two
An Abrupt and Profound Loss of Innocence

The next morning I managed to make the correct turn, found the right highway, and rolled across the Bend bridge. All that I now know about that bridge I learned from Bob Fiedler. The last time I'd covered the same ground, it had been raining. Today, the sun shone through clean cumulous clouds. The corn wasn't nearly as high; it was a month earlier in the season than it was when I'd been here before. The ominous, oppressive feeling I'd had then had been replaced by a sense of peaceful homecoming.

The big red barn and the white clapboard house were unchanged. I pulled into the yard, following the gravel driveway around to the side of the house, then waited for the Fiedlers.

When they pulled up in their truck, a tall, thin man got out and shook my hand, introducing himself as Bob and his wife as Rosella. I was glad to dispense with the formalities. I felt like I already knew them.

Bob, who in his seventies is as spry as a man a quarter of a century his junior, unlocked the house, grabbed some lawn chairs from the covered back porch, and sat us down in the shade of a huge sycamore tree to talk about ancestry.

He was interested in my genealogy, and seemed continually amazed that I am the great-granddaughter of Bertha Gifford. I understood. In some ways, I am continually amazed about that fact myself.

An hour or so later, a car pulled into the drive. It was Bob's son. Tim Fiedler is tall and thin like his father, and equally personable. He pulled up a lawn chair and we began again to discuss the descent of my DNA. Tim, though, was more interested in Bertha.

"Why do you think she did it?" he asked. "I mean, what was her motive for killing all those people?"

"Well…." I told him slowly what I had learned from studying the accounts of her trial. He asked me all the same questions I had asked myself.

Had she really intended a confession when making her statement?

Were there no eye witnesses?

Had the prosecuting attorney had enough evidence to make a case against her?

Why didn't Bertha testify in her own defense?

Why wasn't Dr. Hemker ever held accountable in some way?

How could those St. Louis psychiatrists be so sure, given the circumstances, that Bertha was incurably insane?

I had answers for some of his questions. Others, I will never be able to answer. But at some point deep into our conversation, I became aware of the surrealism of the moment; here was the great-grandson of the man who had allegedly been murdered, sitting with the great-granddaughter of the supposed murderer, discussing in calm detail the merits of the case. Tim and I sat facing each other, the distance between us less than three feet. Certainly if we had been alive seventy-five years before, we would never had had the same conversation. Even now, the mention of Bertha Gifford can evoke anger in individuals who, in 1928, had yet to be born.

The shade cast by the sycamore tree had shifted considerably by the time Bob Fiedler said, "Well, do you want to see the inside of the house?" Tim came along for the tour but Rosella remained outside, comfortable in her lawn chair.

I don't know what I thought I might feel in wandering those rooms. There was nothing to learn, nothing to discover. I couldn't feel nostalgic; I'd never been there. I'd never read a description of the rooms or seen a photograph as I had with the courtroom. As it was, I didn't feel much of anything beyond a vague interest.

We entered through the kitchen and I might have tried to imagine Bertha there, but Bob explained that the entire kitchen area had been remodeled. The Fiedlers often stay in the house on the weekends, so there is a bed in the front bedroom. That's the room where Ed Brinley died. I stopped there, but didn't say anything to Bob or Tim. I again had the sense of arriving just a few minutes too late to change the outcome of a perilous situation.

We continued on, and Bob took me up the narrow stairs to show me the second floor and the attic room. I told him that when my mother had lived here, she and Jim had taken the mule upstairs one day.

"Why?" He sounded as perplexed as if I'd told him they'd built a trout pond in the basement.

"I suppose because they were bored kids and there were no grown-ups around," I said.

When my mother had first told me that story, it surprised me—not because it was such an outrageous thing to do, but because my brother and sister and I had done the exact same thing when we were kids. We didn't have a two-story house, but on more than one occasion we had led my sister's Shetland pony up the back steps and through the kitchen into the carpeted living room, just so she could hang out with us. I told Bob Fiedler this.

"Well, that's one thing," he said, "but a mule is a lot bigger than a Shetland pony…." True enough.

And, I thought, there has to be some significance in the fact that our minds were capable of conceiving the same kind of mischief our mother had gotten into. But at that moment and under those circumstances, I didn't want to dwell too much on inherited traits.

Bob and Tim took me down to the cellar, still braced by its original logs, the bark still visible on them after a hundred years. Then we walked across the yard to look at the old red barn. Bertha had said there were rats in the barn. She told the druggist she needed to buy arsenic because of the rats. I knew now that was a lie. But what was it she didn't want to disclose? Did she lie about the rats because she didn't want old "Doc" Powers to suspect that she intended to commit murder? Or was she simply reluctant to admit that she took the arsenic herself so that she could stay young looking?

"Bertha said she bought the arsenic to take care of the rats in the barn," I said as we approached the large sliding door.

"I've never seen a rat in this barn," Bob said, "and I've been coming out to the farm for over fifty years." I didn't doubt him. Tim slid the door back, and we walked inside.

Later, on the phone, I told my mother about going inside the house and into the barn.

"I had a place for my horse inside that barn," was all she said, but she had a tone in her voice of longing and disappointment. I had come to understand that all her life, she had felt sorry for what had happened there, and sad for what might have been if she could have continued to live on the farm with the grandmother who had been so kind to her. Though she would never articulate those feelings, I knew that she had always carried with her a sense of loss. I had felt it all my life. Learning about Bertha had helped me understand why. What my mother experienced was more than just the loss of whatever warmth and acceptance Bertha offered her as a mother figure. It was an abrupt and profound loss of innocence. Imagine the person you love most in the world. Then imagine being told that while that person was extending love and affection toward you, she had been murdering members of your community. Now imagine you were ten when all of this happened. You might not have understood all the words that the grown-ups were using, but you certainly would have understood their sense of secrecy and shame. And for the rest of your life, how would you ever fully trust anyone? Would you look into the eyes of your loved ones and wonder if things were really as they seemed to be?

These experiences change us. They redirect and define our identities. The young innocent Ernestine who wanted nothing more than to spend her days reading, fishing, and riding her horse in the warmth of the peaceful countryside returned to the cold winter of

Detroit hiding a secret shame as if it were a pregnancy out of wedlock, only this secret would not be surreptitiously born or gotten rid of; it would continue to fester inside of her for decades, and it would keep her always wary, always a measure reticent and sharp-edged, not just with strangers, but also—and especially—with those who loved her.

Chapter Twenty-Three
"A Very Private Funeral"

The kindness of the Fiedlers in those hours I spent with them amounted to more than hospitality. They were genuinely interested in my story because it fascinated them, but also because it was part of their family history as well. Beyond that, they were simply nice people, and I was amazed when I finally got ready to leave that I had been there at the farm for nearly five hours.

The visit itself, the conversation in which we shared what we knew and still didn't know, the tour of the house and the barn—all of these things I will cherish forever. But Bob Fiedler gave me something else that day. And as the value of knowledge often outweighs the value of experience, what he gave me became the greatest gift of that day.

It was a 1981 issue of *St. Louis Magazine*. In it was a thoroughly researched feature article on Bertha Gifford written by a Mr. Joe Popper.

"There are a few inaccuracies," Bob told me as he handed it to me, "but you can probably find those." He had agreed to let me borrow the magazine so that I could get the article photocopied. I would return it to him before I left to go home.

I said good-bye to Bob and Rosella and Tim, knowing I'd see them again in a day or two, and headed back to the motel, where I put my feet up and began to read Popper's article, "A Darkness 'Round the Bend."

I will say this: The man did his homework. In an impressive display of journalistic integrity, he scoured not only the *St. Louis Dispatch*, but also issues of a tiny newspaper that was local to Pacific and Catawissa, the *Pacific Transcript* which, by 1981, had become the *Meramec Valley Transcript*. To his credit, Popper spent hours in the basement of the *Transcript* offices, sifting through ancient issues of the paper dating through an entire decade, searching for tidbits on Bertha and Gene Gifford, or anyone identified as one of her victims.

Also laudable was his attempt to find individuals still living in the area who had been alive during the time of Bertha's arrest and trial. Most were in their seventies and eighties, but they remembered people and events of the time in vivid detail:

> Bertha reminded me of what I used to think an old witch would look like. She was wearing this awful black dress and had something strange and black on her head. And she was acting in the most peculiar way, kind of sneaking around the room like she was trying to hear what people were saying. She knew there was talk.

****

> She was a wonderful cook, I'll say that, one of the best biscuit bakers in the county. She seemed like a nice person, though one day she'd be this way, one day she'd be that way. I mean, her mood would change from real sweet to kind of feisty. She was sort of a good-looking woman with dark hair and a dark complexion. Not very tall….
>
> Anyone got sick, she was right there. She'd run right over with her satchel. She always wore a white apron when she came to call. Later on, I think she started to wear a regular nurse's outfit. She was

always meticulously clean. She could be so friendly, so warm....

The article itself was, for the most part, accurate, though the writer did tend to embellish somewhat. He wrote of Bertha's agitated state in the jail, "as she paced back and forth, howling like a wolf, and making other ungodly noises" and "the times she stood holding the bars of her cell window, shouting horrid curses at the darkened street below," but he didn't substantiate these depictions as being eye witness accounts or drawn from newspaper descriptions.

The majority of Popper's article focused on Bertha's relationship with her community—and the gruesomeness of her victims' deaths. He gave a brief account of her trial and stated, "The trial revealed nothing. But it was good theatre and it served its purpose. The growth had been removed." And he included a short description of what it's like to die from arsenic poisoning:

> Severe gastrointestinal pain is experienced within an hour or so after the poison is taken. This is generally followed by a burning sensation around the lips, a tightening of the throat and increasing difficulty in swallowing. The next symptom is excruciating pain accompanied by spasmodic vomiting. Other symptoms include severe headache, vertigo, stupor, blurring of vision, muscle cramping, atrophy and coma. Death may come within 60 minutes but usually takes longer."

The additional material included the history of arsenic's use:

> In more recent times it was used as a treatment for venereal disease and various forms of parasite infestation. It was also a popular component of over-the-counter health tonics because of its cosmetic effect. In very low doses, ingested over a long period

of time, arsenic can produce a "peaches and cream"
or "milk and roses" complexion because it causes the
blood vessels of the skin to dilate.

Popper provided background for his piece that would enable the
reader to establish a clear perspective of time and place:
It was a very different time then and that is
important to remember. Otherwise the things I'm
going to tell you won't make much sense. It was an
age of patent medicines and gravel-top roads, of
Hupmobiles and Marmons, Hudsons and Chandlers
and a president named Coolidge. Phonographs were
advertised as "talking machines," boarding house
owners sought "clean Protestant men" …Al Smith
and Herbert Hoover were squaring off, the country
was still officially "dry," the Depression was more
than a year away and a Sunday drive to St. Louis
from the outlying town of Pacific was a major
event—all the more so if you made it without at least
one flat tire. Towns now considered St. Louis
suburbs were far from the city then, and the
countryside was farther still.

The journalist's take on Bertha Gifford was without doubt that she
was a "killer," and his opening set the tone for an eerie, macabre tale:
It was unseasonably cool during the early
morning hours of August 25, 1928, but Andrew
McDonnell, the police chief of Webster Groves, was
sweating as he drove. Not profusely, mind you, he
was a pro; just enough to uncomfortably remind him
of his own anxiety. He was heading north that
morning toward a small farm outside the town of
Eureka where he intended to make an arrest, an

unusual arrest, perhaps the most important of his career. He didn't know what to expect.

But there were no problems. The arrest came off without a hitch. He took into custody a leaden-eyed 53-year-old woman who offered no resistance and seemed more confused than afraid or angry. Her passive reaction, while a relief, struck McDonnell as unusual since he had informed her that she was charged with murder, first degree, two counts. She merely brushed it aside and wondered aloud why anyone would say such a thing about her. The victims listed in the warrant McDonnell carried were a middle-aged farm hand and a seven-year-old boy. This, too, struck him as odd for they had so little in common. Almost nothing, really, except that they had both known the woman. That was the only real link. That and the way they died.

The article was entertaining and deftly written, providing a greater dimension to the lives and times of the people involved. (George Schamel played outfield for the Catawissa baseball team and was their best batter. Bertha and Gene Gifford held a dinner party in their home just before Christmas in 1922.) But the only significant piece of information for me came in the very last paragraph:

Bertha Gifford spent nearly 23 years in Farmington. She died there on August 20, 1951. Gene arranged to have her body brought to Pacific for a very private funeral. She is buried in Morse Mill cemetery. Her grave is unmarked. The undertaker's records show that the service and burial cost $266.69 and that Gene put down $166.69. The balance is marked "unpaid."

Finally, I could tell my mother where her grandmother was buried.

The next morning I headed south through the countryside to Morse Mill. I found the small town easily—using the map Mom and I had purchased nine years before. The cemetery is on a hill right next to the highway, adjacent to the Church of God Faith of Abraham. This is the church that Bertha's parents belonged to when they were alive.

After I parked the truck, I walked slowly up the gravel drive past the church. The first headstone visible when you enter the cemetery is the one that marks the grave of Sherman Pounds. His wife lies next to him. These were the great-grandparents of Tim Fiedler.

Less than fifty feet away stands a huge old mulberry tree with branches that hang nearly to the ground and provide cool, dense shade. At the base of the tree is the grave of Eugene Gifford. I was shocked to find it. Mom told me later that she had never known where Gene was buried. I took a picture to take back to her. It seemed like such a peaceful place.

There is a line of graves next to Gene's—his mother and his younger brother James. Both of them were possible victims of Bertha's poisoning. They had both died while living in her home. James was only thirteen when he died, and I realized while looking at the dates that Bertha and Gene's son, James—Mom's Uncle Jim— had been born the same year Gene's brother had died. The baby named for the brother lost.

Directly behind Gene's grave there is a marker for another grave. It's a foundation, really, for a headstone, so the top is rough with nothing engraved on it. I am sure that it is Bertha's grave. And I am just as sure that the one hundred dollar balance which Gene owed and never paid was meant to cover the cost of a headstone, but since he died before he could pay it, the headstone was never completed. Gene would have never intentionally left her grave unmarked.

I stepped back to take more pictures for my mother, to get a more panoramic view, and had to step around a very large headstone that was out in front of all the others. I glanced at the engraving. It marked the grave of Henry Graham, Bertha's first husband, and, I realized, my mother's grandfather. She had never known him. A second later, of course, I realized that this would be my great-grandfather.

There is a sense of history that comes to you in a place like this, a sense of permanence and a sense of perspective. Henry and Bertha no doubt bought the large plot in the cemetery after they were married. When Henry died, it became Bertha's—and her next husband's, when they married. Gene set aside a place for himself, buried his mother and his brother and a few other relatives there, had Bertha buried there when she passed, and was finally laid among them himself. This would doubtless never happen in the rapidly changing world we live in today with our astronomical divorce rate and our acceptance of serial monogamy. It was, indeed, a different time back then.

Now here they all were. They had shared joys and sorrows, kindness and cruelty. At the end of it, they were all gathered together.

A thought crossed my mind. Bertha's maiden name was Williams. She had been born here in Morse Mill, so chances are her kin had been buried here. I strolled slowly through the tall grass toward another large group of headstones and sure enough, here was the rest of the clan. I took some time simply to peruse the history and names of my ancestry and to take some pictures to share with my mother.

I had expected this day to feel sadness, as I had when I'd gone to Ed Brinley's grave. But I didn't. I felt peace which came from knowing, finally, that there is an end to suffering, that no matter what happens to us in this world, no matter what agonies we endure, there is an end to the anguish that is inherent in being human, there is a cessation of that physical humanness, and a liberation which occurs—however we want to envision it.

And I felt, more intensely than any other emotion, the presence of forgiveness. I didn't need to know what had happened any more. Death provided the ultimate ending for all of those whose lives had been affected by the actions of my great-grandmother, including herself; all had passed on to a better place, rendering the truth irrelevant.

Chapter Twenty-Four
"That's All That's Left of It"

My story could end right here. I had set out, years ago, to discover the extent of Bertha's guilt or innocence, only to find that now it matters not at all. With my realization that all of the suffering had passed, I gained a new perspective on my own personal suffering. In a very tangible way, I no longer felt alone in the world. And that, in itself, would be a terrific ending—except the story was still unfolding.

If you do an internet search for Bertha Gifford, you'll come across a website that showcases Morse Mill, Missouri as the "City of the Month" for Jefferson County. (The designation was made and the material posted in June of 1999, but as of this writing it remains online.) The pages offer a brief, interesting history of the small community and some photographs. Credit is given to one Alice Lee, postmaster of Morse Mill, for providing historical background and information on the town's "most infamous resident"—Bertha Gifford.

The day I visited the cemetery in Morse Mill was a Saturday, and although I drove down later and found the post office, it was closed. So I returned two days later, on Monday, in an attempt to find Alice Lee. Most of the information she had given on the internet site had been accurate, including the fact that Bertha eventually became a cook at Farmington. (Two facts invariably emerge when talking to people who know about her: She was 'once beautiful,' and she was a good cook. Apparently the administrators at the institution trusted her enough to allow her to do what she did best—and didn't seem to fear that there might be dire consequences in doing so.)

I was hoping that Alice Lee might tell me more about Bertha and her family, but when I stopped in at the post office I learned that she had retired. The current postmaster, Beth Ryan, was, like so many others had been, warm, friendly and helpful. She took my card and promised to give it to Alice if she came by the post office, which she was known to do on a regular basis. I told Beth I would be leaving for California the next day, so she'd have to call me there. I hoped she would.

There wasn't much left for me to do in Missouri. I had returned Bob Fiedler's copy of St. Louis magazine, having made photocopies of Joe Popper's article (one of which I immediately sent to my mother). Seeing Bob and Rosella again had given me the opportunity to sit once again beneath the big sycamore tree and talk to them about the importance of knowing from whence we come—not because it necessarily makes a difference as to who we are, but because it makes a difference in how we feel about ourselves.

In hindsight, I know that my almost frantic desire to see the farmhouse and other places Bertha had been was driven by my need to try to 'solve the mystery,' to determine whether or not my great-grandmother was a murderer. But as I realized that day in the graveyard, those issues have meaning only for those of us who are here now and are curious, not for those who were here then and have been released from the horror of it.

There were two things I needed to accomplish, though, before I left Missouri.

After I left the post office in Morse Mill that day, I continued driving south to the Southeast Missouri Mental Health Center. It is approximately seventy miles from Catawissa to Farmington. I'd learned from reading Joe Popper's article that Gene and Bertha Gifford, a few years before her arrest, had had a productive year raising hogs, and Gene had used the surplus money they made to buy a brand new Essex automobile. As I drove my truck down to

Farmington on the highway—most of the time obeying the sixty-mile-per-hour speed limit—I wondered what it would have been like for Gene, slowly tooling along in his Essex over those old gravel roads. It would have taken him several hours each way. There is no doubt in my mind that he felt it was worth it to see the woman he loved.

The mental health center is now contained within a beautiful modern building. If the original building where Bertha was housed still exists, it is impossible to see it behind the fortress-like structure which sprawls across the front of the property now. Just to see what would happen, I went inside and told the receptionist that I needed information on a patient who had died there in 1951. She smiled, asked me to have a seat in the lobby, and called a representative from the records department to 'come out' and speak to me. (Doors to all the administrative offices are locked. The receptionist spoke to me from behind very thick glass.)

The middle-aged woman who approached me introduced herself and asked if she could help. I explained that my great-grandmother had lived there for twenty-three years and had died there, and I asked if I could look at her records.

"Not without a court order," she told me.

I explained to her that I lived in California, that I was only in Missouri for a brief period of time, that my mother, who had been raised by her grandmother, had never been advised as to what had happened to her during her incarceration or after her death. I told her I just wanted a chance to look through her file to see if it contained anything I might pass on to my mother. By this time, she was shaking her head continuously.

"I couldn't give you any information whatsoever unless you demonstrated to the court that you are an executor of her estate."

One has to wonder how much of an estate the resident of a state-funded mental hospital who died over fifty years ago might have. But one learns not to argue when it is glaringly apparent that doing so would be futile.

I told her I appreciated her time, and I left.

When I got back in my truck, I said thank you—aloud—to whomever it was who had sent me those photocopies of Bertha's file. I understood clearly why the woman had done so without identifying herself. I will be forever grateful.

The one last thing I hadn't succeeded in doing was finding the jail in Union where Bertha had been incarcerated during those long weeks between her arrest in August and the November trial. Over the week that I stayed in Pacific, I had asked people on several occasions if they knew where the county jail might have been. No one that I asked seemed to know.

When I arrived back at the motel after my visit to Farmington, it was late in the day. I would be leaving for California the next day, so I packed up my things and went to bed early in order to get an early start. Before I fell asleep the thought occurred to me to contact the Chamber of Commerce in Union. Over the years as a writer (and sometimes as a tourist), I have found that one of the best sources of information in any city is its Chamber of Commerce. As a general rule, whoever answers the phone is someone familiar with the town in which they live and the people who live in it, and if they don't have the answer to something, they know who does.

Such was the case the next morning when I called the Union Chamber of Commerce and asked about the jail. I was given the number of Kevin Mooney, who is the city's historian. I caught him in the middle of a bite of toast when I called. When I apologized he told me it was good that I had called since he and his family were leaving on vacation momentarily.

The jail, he said, was at the top of the courthouse.

That's why the writer for the Post-Dispatch had talked about her being in the "upper tier." He'd meant the top story of the courthouse. In the long weeks between her arrest and her trial, Bertha had occupied a cell on the third story of the courthouse—until the night before her trial. I learned later that she stayed at the Central Hotel (which still stands) in Union for the duration of the trial, presumably to make herself look presentable to the public each day in court. She was given three meals a day while there—breakfast, dinner and supper. The total bill for three days of room and board was $58.50. So while she did spend her weeks awaiting trial in the jail cell of the courthouse, she was escorted (by Sheriff Gorg, we can assume) to the courthouse each day of her trial and led around to the side of the building where there is a nondescript steel door which opens to a narrow inner staircase, leading up to the single courtroom. I have no doubt that Sheriff Gorg, who seemed sympathetic toward her in newspaper accounts, would have carefully taken her arm to help her up any and all steps.

Kevin Mooney continued his fascinating history to note that if the jury had found Bertha Gifford guilty, she would have been hanged right there in the courthouse. When it was built in 1922, the architects designed an indoor gallows.

"Oh yeah," Kevin told me, "when I was a kid, we used to take field trips to the courthouse and they'd take us up to the top and show it to us. It was never used, though." *Almost*, I thought.

Kevin assured me that if I stopped in at the courthouse, Bill Miller, the Circuit Court Clerk, would show me the jail and the gallows.

So, with the truck packed, I headed west on 44, pulling off the highway for the short drive into Union. Parking in front of the courthouse, I double-checked my camera to make sure it had a fresh roll of film. This would make my last day in Missouri memorable.

When I found Bill Miller and asked him about the jail, he confirmed what Kevin had said, though he seemed a bit hesitant. He'd already left his desk and was walking me down the hall as we spoke. I asked him if I could see the jail.

"Well…" he answered, opening a door that led to an inner hallway and gesturing me through, "I could…." He opened a second door ahead of me and again I walked through it. We stood in the center of a brightly lit, nicely furnished office. Several clerks were busy typing, filing and answering the phone.

"It was right here," he said. "After they built the new jail, they needed more room in the courthouse, so they plastered over the walls of the old jail and made it into office space."

So much for cement floors, iron bars, and the image of my great-grandmother huddled in a corner with a blanket over her head. I asked Bill if the gallows had been covered over during the renovation.

"That's all that's left of it," he said, pointing to the ceiling. Just above our heads was a clearly defined trapdoor which appeared entirely incongruous in the current environment.

Maybe it's just my peculiar sense of humor (we should, I suppose, consider my ancestry), but the thought of those clerks and secretaries working diligently on court business every day while directly overhead looms the trapdoor of a gallows just struck me as funny. I was still laughing as I got in the truck and headed back to Highway 44 to start my journey home.

Chapter Twenty-Five
"Some Kind of Cousins"

By the time I called Beth Ryan, I'd been back home in California for a week. I had decided on the long drive home that I wanted to see about paying the outstanding balance Gene had owed on Bertha's burial and also about having a headstone placed on her grave. My thought was that Beth, as postmaster in Morse Mill, would know most of the folks who lived and did business there, and she might be able to put me in touch with the custodian of the cemetery.

She remembered me when I called. Unfortunately, she couldn't tell me who managed the cemetery. She didn't live in Morse Mill and hadn't been Postmaster long enough to get to know everyone yet.

"Has Alice Lee called you?" she asked after we had talked awhile. I told her I hadn't heard from her but would like to, just to swap stories on Bertha Gifford.

"Oh dear," Beth said. She sounded hesitant. She told me she'd given Mrs. Lee my card and my message the day after I'd stopped in at the post office.

"When I told her it was about Bertha Gifford, she sounded...upset. I think her family was...affected."

I wasn't surprised. Each of the small towns like Morse Mill, Catawissa, Robertsville and Pacific had a handful of families which grew to populate each area. Cousins married cousins, and everyone ended up related to everyone else eventually, either by blood or by marriage. The chances of Alice Lee having a family member who died while in the care of my great-grandmother were great.

I thanked Beth for passing on my message and told her I would keep in touch.

Several days later my phone rang.

"Is this Kay Murphy?" There was a slight edge to the caller's voice. "This is Alice Lee."

I understood immediately why she had seemed agitated when Beth Ryan had given her my message. Her mother-in-law, Hazel Lee— Hazel Pounds Lee—was the sister of Beulah Pounds. Mrs. Lee herself is the niece of Sherman Pounds.

Alice Lee is a treasure. She is a straightforward woman who doesn't hesitate to say what's on her mind, and she is filled with stories and folklore regarding the history and people of Morse Mill. I was amazed to hear that she and her husband own and are renovating a cabin built by Bertha's father, William Poindexter Williams. She told me that there had been opposing views for generations as to who actually built the cabin, John Morse, founder of Morse Mill, or my great-great-grandfather. When she and her husband began their remodeling project, they tore out the old doorframe—and found a length of wood with "W. P. Williams" carved into it, ending the argument once and for all.

Initially Alice Lee seemed skeptical of my relationship to Bertha Gifford. She may be skeptical still. Eventually, though, she told me, "Well, if you're a Williams, you should talk to Jean Thompson. Her grandfather was a Williams."

This was something I hadn't expected. It had never occurred to me that I might have living relatives on my mother's side of the family. My Irish Catholic father was one of seven siblings; I have more cousins than I can count, and we can trace our generations back at least a couple of centuries to their county of origin in Ireland. My mother's family, however, was scattered even before Bertha Gifford's time of infamy, and certainly afterward became fragmented by divorce and relocated by distance and alienation. I had assumed that James Gifford, Bertha and Gene's son, had been the last descendant from Morse Mill. Little did I know….

Alice Lee gave me Jean Thompson's phone number and address. Before we ended our conversation, I asked her who the caretaker of the Morse Mill cemetery might be.

"Well, I was in charge of it for years," she told me. "Now it's managed by my son-in-law." Alice would put me in touch with him so that I could arrange for Bertha's headstone.

It took me several days to prepare myself to call Jean Thompson, to figure out what I would say. After all, I had no idea how family members, this many generations hence, might feel about Bertha Gifford's scandalous behavior.

Of course, I needn't have waited. As soon as I mentioned that I'd gotten her number from Alice Lee, Jean and I had a connection in common. (And an even greater connection than I realized; I would later learn from Jean that the Williams clan had married into the Pounds clan generations ago. Alice and I were distant cousins.) I told Jean that I was Bertha Gifford's great-granddaughter.

"Bertha Gifford! Oh my lord!" She was laughing in spite of her exclamation, a reaction I would not have anticipated. "Well, if you're Bertha's great-granddaughter and I'm her brother's granddaughter, that makes us…."

"Cousins?" I supplied, though I had no idea how to trace the lineage. She laughed again, a deep, resonating laugh.

"Well, we're some kind of cousins!" She sounded as excited as I was to make contact. We began to tell each other stories.

As it turns out, Jean has been studying the genealogy of the Williams family for years. She was able to tell me the names of Bertha's parents and siblings, where they lived, who their children were…and their children's children. In turn, I told her how I was the daughter of Bertha's granddaughter, and that my mother had been living with Bertha at the time of her arrest.

"Where was James?" she asked.

"James?"

"James Gifford, Gene's son. We always wondered what happened to him. No one in the family ever knew. We knew he left town after she went to the mental hospital, but he just disappeared after that. I've been looking for that boy for years."

I had to laugh. Jean referred to Mom's Uncle Jim as a "boy" because he had left Catawissa at the age of fourteen, right after his mother was sent to Farmington, just as she had said. This was a part of the story that I knew firsthand from my mother, so I was able to help Jean fill in a missing piece in the jigsaw of her—our—family.

Jim had left town, angry, ashamed and embarrassed by his mother. He drifted for awhile after he left Franklin County, trying to find odd jobs to support himself. Eventually, he made his way up to Michigan and came to stay awhile with my mother and grandmother in Detroit. Eventually he joined the Civilian Conservation Corps which took him to California, where he found work on a ranch in San Luis Obispo. Some time later, he married the ranch owner's daughter. He and Lucille had several children who are still living. James Gifford died in 1985 at the age of seventy-one.

Jean Thompson turned her face away from the phone and called to her husband in another room.

"Hey Slim! I found out what happened to James! He went to California!" And to me she said, "We always wondered what happened to that boy! Now we know!"

It didn't matter to her, of course, that she'd never met James, that she was born twenty-four years after he was born, ten years after he'd left Catawissa. James Gifford was a family member, regardless of the passing of time or the separation of distance.

In the conversations we've had and the letters we've exchanged since then, Jean has made me feel this way, too, like a long-lost cousin coming home. In a very real sense, I am.

Perhaps the most ironic of the connections I've made has been with the youngest daughter of Ed Brinley. When I was in the midst of making all my discoveries, I shared some of them with my brother's wife, who at the time was working on our family's genealogy. She was fascinated by the story of Bertha, and she wrote to the St. Louis Post-Dispatch, asking for copies of the photos they had of her on file. When the newspaper learned that I was working on a book, a reporter called and asked for an interview. The subsequent article was accurate overall, but there were a few things that the reporter hadn't heard correctly over the phone. When I emailed her to let her know, she admitted that the daughter of Ed Brinley had contacted her as well, because she was upset at the characterization of her father as "the town drunk." (Remember, this was my mother's description, not mine.) I felt remorse for having passed on the unkind phrase, but was thrilled at the same time that a relative of Ed Brinley was still living. I asked the reporter to have the woman contact me so that I could apologize, and so that she would have the opportunity to set the record straight about her father before the book was published. Some days later I received a very gracious letter from LaVerne Brinley Sheppard. She was ten when Bertha was tried for the murder of her father. She remembered the trial. She sent her phone number, and I called her. I told her about my afternoon in the Brush Creek Cemetery, about sitting among the Brinley headstones and crying for the children who, like me, had lost their father at a young age, and I told her how sorry I was for her loss. She in turn told me wonderful stories about her father, how he used to take her fishing, and how kind he was as a father, and certainly did not fit the stereotype of "town drunk." I thought of my own father, his fishing trips with my brothers, and his drinking, which nearly caused my parents to separate. I told LaVerne that we'd had very similar experiences, and that I felt very connected to her. "That doesn't surprise me," she responded, "since we're cousins." This was when I learned that Bertha Gifford and Ed Brinley were third cousins. Later, LaVerne would send me an extensive genealogy of the Brinley family, and I could trace our familial connection for myself. I had already determined long before that Ed Brinley, however he was characterized by others, deserved far better than the hand he'd been dealt. The warm relationship I've established with LaVerne continues with great fondness, and it has made me even more conscious of Bertha's victims as innocent individuals whose memories deserve to be validated and respected.

Chapter Twenty-Six
Missouri-Farmwife-and-Kind-Grandmother-Turned-Serial-Killer

Not surprisingly, I often talk to people about my great-grandmother, and the question I'm asked most frequently is this: "Why do you think she did it?" I don't recall anyone ever asking me, "Do you think she really did it?" The truth is, what makes a more provocative story is the Missouri-farmwife-and-kind-grandmother-turned-serial-killer slant. I know some readers have come to this book in search of that very aspect and if you have, dear reader, you may have been disappointed—but hang on—I have two more scintillating tidbits to tell.

First, though, I want to say this: When a story of this nature is revealed, it can never be fully exposed; some part of it, because of circumstances or the passing of time, will always remain veiled. We may speculate about what the whole story might be, but we can never know for certain if we're right. One thing I do know for sure is that, in general, people see only what they want to see. This is entirely a matter of choice. Thus, if I chose to see Bertha Gifford as a murderous, psychopathic monster, I could catalyze that image in my mind and never alter it, seeing only those nuances in the evidence presented which would support my view. Or, if I chose to believe that my great-grandmother was the victim of circumstance, of mass hysteria in a small town, I could build a case for that. I could even make the argument that she was the scapegoat for an aging and drug-addicted Dr. Hemker, if I were to so choose. My point is that what I might say makes very little difference; those who have made up their minds in regard to her guilt or innocence have already done so. Any statement I might make will do little to sway them. Having said all that, let me now offer my opinion. Did she give arsenic to sick people? Yes. I don't think anyone would debate that. She went all the way to Pacific on the morning of the day Ed Brinley died—without telling Gene where she was going— just to buy rat poison, even though she had a man lying ill in the front bedroom of her house. It's obvious that her intention in buying it was to administer some of it to him. Likewise, I'm certain that she gave arsenic to others over the years. I have seen the pages of Doc Powers' old ledger—it still exists—with Bertha's signature written again and again to document that she had purchased arsenic.

However, one point that never seems to be considered is this: How many community members did she care for who recovered from their illnesses? These people lived in a time before antibiotics and refrigeration. Bacterial infections, including botulism, salmonella and other food-related toxins, were a way of life. Children and the elderly succumbed frequently. What number of people were sick in Bertha's community over the sixteen-year period in which she was a volunteer nurse? If she cared for two hundred over that period of time, or roughly one a month, and seventeen of them died, that seems to be a mortality rate which might be expected, given the time period and the circumstances. But if she cared for twenty or twenty-five and seventeen of those died—well, the handful who survived must have felt quite blessed. It seems more likely that if she showed up to nurse anyone and everyone who became ill, as her community members kept reiterating, then, in that length of time spanning a decade and a half, she must have cared for quite a significant number. There's no way to know how many she gave arsenic to, but I suspect it was quite a few.

So the question is, when she gave arsenic to them, did she do so with the intention of killing them? My potentially biased and nonprofessional opinion is no, she did not—with one exception. I am neither a psychiatrist nor an expert on serial killers (though I did spend a disturbing amount of time studying them as research for this book). But I have been a student of human behavior all my life. I don't believe that Bertha Gifford wanted Ed Brinley or the Schamel boys or others she might have poisoned to die. I do think she wanted to make them very, very sick.

After talking to Alice Lee and Jean Thompson, it is clear that everyone knew Bertha was not to be trusted. Long before Ed Brinley's estranged wife pestered the authorities into holding an inquest, family members, friends and neighbors had begun to be watchful around Bertha. They knew she was poisoning people and, of course, no one wanted to be the next victim.

Jean Thompson, whose grandfather was Bertha's brother, told me a story that had been passed down in her family about something which happened after her grandparents had moved to Kansas. Jean's father, a young boy at the time, recalled an incident that occurred when "Aunt Berthie" came to visit. The women were in the kitchen cooking, and the children went out to play. When they did, they found a tin out in the yard that they'd never seen before. Opening it, they found a white powder inside. They ran to the house with it to show it to the grown-ups and Jean's grandmother tossed the powder into the stove to destroy it.

"They knew it was probably poison," Jean said. "Bertha probably put it out there for one of the kids to find and get sick so she could nurse him back to health 'cause that's what she did."

Why didn't anyone say anything? It may seem odd to us now on the face of it, but in those days if a family member was 'not right in the head' the issue was not considered a topic for discussion in polite society. Time and time again I've heard, "You just didn't talk about it." And while this might seem horrific considering the consequences, have we really evolved all that much in seventy-five years? I can tell you from my perspective that we have not. We do not talk openly in my family about my struggle with depression. We do not talk about it at all. Some of my writing has touched on suicide and my personal experiences but I've never discussed these things with anyone in my family, nor with any of my close friends. It's understandable; no one wants to be the one to broach the subject. Let's face it: There is no comfortable, light-hearted way to ask someone if she is feeling particularly suicidal. And yet consider the consequences....

The Williams family and others in the community had realized that Bertha would sometimes poison people, though they might not have known how. Their response was to accept that as some demented idiosyncrasy and simply try to prevent it by being aware of it. For better or worse, she was a member of their society, and they were reluctant, until Ludelphia Brinley, to send her away.

The story of Bertha leaving poison out for the children carried with it two important facts: family knowledge of her proclivity and motive. Yes, they knew, but no one said anything. And they suspected she did it so that she could then make the sick person well and thus become the hero. Weighing all that I know about the facts, about certain familial personality traits, and about human behavior in general, this is what I believe as well. When Bertha gave arsenic to the Schamel boys and to Ed Brinley, I don't think she ever intended for them to die. I would love to make myself believe that she had seen Doc Hemker administer arsenic to help patients get better so she did the same thing herself, innocently believing that she was 'helping them,' as she had claimed. But the evidence and logic both dictate that this was not the case. She knew that the arsenic she gave them would produce violent illness, and she gave it to them anyway with the intention of sitting with them throughout the ordeal, caring for them, comforting them, and so garnering the gratitude, the praise, the hero-worship of the entire community. In short, she would not only be accepted within the society in which she lived, she would be respected.

This is, in fact, exactly what happened...in the beginning. Bertha, who had been criticized and talked about for 'keeping company' with a man ten years her junior while still married to her first husband, who was too attractive (often a deficit in a small town) and too outspoken, who could be charming one minute and volatile the next, Bertha, with her fifth grade education and her remarriage to Gene Gifford in less than a year after her husband's death—this was the same woman who became known far and wide as the Good Samaritan, the woman who could be counted on to travel any distance at any time to reach a community member who had fallen ill, sitting up with them, often refusing to eat herself, until the patient recovered—or died.

Chances are, in the beginning, she didn't use arsenic. Maybe someone got sick and Bertha, out of guilt or shame or an overwhelming need to redeem herself in the eyes of society, sat by the sick one's bedside selflessly until that person was well again. If she were praised or thanked or received any recognition for this at all, the behavior would have been reinforced. It's possible that this is what triggered her compulsion to voluntarily care for any sick member of the community. Though she did not wear a tangible scarlet letter, my great-grandmother had been marked by the society in which she lived, and, like Hester Prynn, she set about to earn her redemption through service to the very community that would ostracize her.

But perhaps at some point, one of her 'patients' wasn't all that sick to begin with. Maybe someone had a cold or other minor ailment, and there was little concern that he would recover...so Bertha gave just a little bit of arsenic, as she had seen Doc Hemker do, knowing that her patient's condition would deteriorate for awhile, but would eventually rally, and the worried family members would be all that much more grateful to her for actually saving a life. If the patient died, of course, that feeling would be negated; she would have failed in her attempt to 'save' the afflicted and thereby the personal satisfaction to her in terms of thanks and admiration would have diminished, so it follows that she would poison them only to cause or exacerbate illness, not with the intention of murder.

And maybe it occurred to her to choose arsenic for this purpose because she had seen what had happened to her husband when she gave some to him. I do think Henry Graham died because she poisoned him with the intention of killing him.

There are three reasons why I believe this. The first is simply intuition. Long before I read in the *St. Louis Post-Dispatch* that others suspected she killed her first husband, I had the distinct feeling that this was probably the case. She wanted to marry Gene…she was angry at Henry for having an affair…obviously her marriage was an unhappy one…. Henry had been sick with pneumonia and was under the treatment of a doctor. Then suddenly his gastrointestinal system was affected, which seems an unlikely complication of the respiratory illness. Add to those facts something else that Jean Thompson had shared with me. Her uncle, Bertha's nephew, had told her (when she finally learned, in middle age, as I did, the family secret of the mad woman in the asylum):

"I know she killed him. I didn't know it then, but I know it now. I never saw a man die a more violent death than Henry Graham."

And, to my mind, there is another indication that Bertha murdered her first husband. Her behavior during her trial when Gene Gifford testified was characteristic of someone with a guilty conscience, as if the two shared the secret of her wrong-doing and she was afraid he would give it away. While every other witness testified, Bertha sat dejected and withdrawn, not fully engaged in what was said or done. In stark contrast, when Gene took the stand, she became agitated, almost fearful—the opposite of what one might expect, since Gene was the only witness who was entirely sympathetic to her, to say nothing of the love he had for her. Even the Post-Dispatch writer took notice:

> Mrs. Gifford betrayed emotion for the first time since the opening of the trial Monday, as Gene—who is 10 years her junior and was 22 when she married him in 1906—took his seat in the witness chair. Her

knuckles were white as she pressed her clenched hands against her mouth. She listened intently, focusing directly on a witness for the first time.

Was she, as she stared at him, willing him not to give away their secret? That she had poisoned Henry Graham so the two could be together? I suspect that is what was behind her terror. She needn't have worried. Gene would never betray her.

The murder of Henry Graham helps to shed more light on Bertha's later behavior. It would explain her obsessive need to redeem herself by caring for the sick. It would also help us understand the breakdown of her moral fabric, how she could begin to allow herself to give poison to innocent victims, because she had done this before and, like any immoral activity, each successive time it becomes a little easier.

Was Bertha insane? The most compelling part of my discussion with Tim Fiedler the day we sat at the farm under the sycamore tree centered around whether a person who commits murder is insane. I think we concluded, after much discussion, that there are two types of murderers—those who commit the crime out of some passion such as anger, betrayal, greed, or fear, and those who murder for the sake of killing. The latter, of course, would be the psychopathic, serial killer type. Although I know that many would disagree with me, I do not think, given my explanation of her need to seek redemption, that Bertha fits this profile. I believe Bertha falls into the first category, that she murdered Henry out of her desire to be with Gene exclusively and perhaps out of her sense of betrayal at Henry's infidelity. For all we know, there were other issues that drove Bertha away from Henry and into the arms of Gene Gifford. I do not believe that her murder of Henry Graham, though it was morally wrong, was the act of a psychotic woman (though there is legal precedent to suggest that she might have had a psychotic episode at the moment she administered the poison which killed him).

Obviously, the state of her mental capacity was altered. This was mostly caused, I think, by the guilt she carried all those years after Henry's death. The psychiatrists at her trial, and later those at Farmington, suggested that she was delusional. Yes, she adopted the persona of a nurse, even donning a nurse's uniform in the years just before she was incarcerated. (In the photo of her taken at Farmington, she is wearing it.) Does that make her delusional? I hesitate to draw that conclusion, considering the fine line between hope and delusion. If we dress and act like what we wish we could be, are we deluding ourselves? If your neighbor who plays in a garage band wears his hair long and has multiple body piercings despite being forty-five years old, should his family call a mental hospital and have him committed? (That one, I suppose, is debatable.) Bertha didn't hallucinate. She never heard voices. She never said anything in her interview with the psychiatrists at Farmington that could be construed as being out of touch with reality.

After she went to Farmington, she became a model inmate. She worked first in the beauty salon, then as a cook in the kitchen. From time to time, she was allowed to go home. She was calm and cooperative. When my mother saw her after she'd been there ten years, she seemed well adjusted. She knew that she was guilty of wrongdoing, that there was a price to pay, and that being in the institution was a consequence of choices she had made. But she also knew, and Gene knew, and, I suspect, many others such as her attorneys and Judge Breuer and Frank Jenny knew, that her incarceration had nothing to do with her being crazy.

Within the sheaf of photocopied documents I received from Farmington, I found a doctor's handwritten notes on her illnesses. Bertha had recurring gall bladder trouble and it caused her frequent episodes of "severe" pain. Across the bottom of one of the medical file forms a note was scrawled, "Probably needs surgery. Family notified of this." That was in April of 1949, two years before she died.

Bertha would have been seventy-five at the time. There is nothing to indicate in any of the documents that the surgery was ever performed, though she did continue to suffer from attacks of nausea and pain.

The last photocopied page is a completed medical form which states, in part: "Patient has paralysis of right arm and leg. Is semi-comatose.... Family notified. Condition critical."

I have read these documents countless times in the years since I received them, and I have never been able to read this last page without feeling desperately sad. Whatever she was, Bertha Gifford was a human being and, to whatever degree, she must have been capable of human feeling; she loved my mother and cared for her as if she were her own daughter. By the time she died in 1951, my mother and father were married and were living in Highland Park, Illinois, with their two little boys—my older brothers. Had Mom only known, I know she would have gone to her grandmother's side and stayed with her to comfort her as she passed away. It is almost a certainty that she died alone.

I have said before but I feel I need to repeat, if only for emphasis, that it is not my intention to vindicate or excuse Bertha Gifford for the crimes she committed. Although that may have been true at the outset of my journey, at some point it became my desire only to try to understand, from an objective point of view, what went on all those years ago, and how it might affect me.

I must say now that the journey has changed me. The legacy of mental illness that I feared to find has not materialized. If anything, I have learned to understand my own response to the world by gaining a more complete understanding of my mother's, and her mother's before her, and her mother's before her. We have all suffered, in one way or another, in one form or another, cruelty, rejection, isolation and betrayal. And we have responded both positively and negatively to those issues, though mostly, it seems, negatively.

Knowing what I know now, I think I can respond more positively. I do not believe in any way that it is my inherited destiny to suffer from mental illness. I do believe that I was born with certain personality traits that will always predispose me to having a deeper, more intense response to emotional pain than others do, perhaps. And this type of pain can, at times, draw me into depression if I am not careful. But I am beginning to see this inherited trait as a boon.

William Wordsworth said that a person with a true poet's heart would have a "heightened sensitivity" to the world at large. If this aspect of my character, this heightened sensitivity, is ultimately what compels me to write, to express those deep feelings in a common language in order to share in the universal experiences of humankind, then it is a gift, and I receive it with joy, because it is my identity, my individual persona…my own opportunity for redemption.

Epilogue

Every summer a farmer in Mission Viejo, here in Southern California, plants a field of corn. When it is grown, he cuts an intricate pattern into it to create a maze and then opens it to the public. The pattern changes every summer. Some years ago, when my kids and I attempted to find our way through, it was cut in the shape of a giant orca and her calf. Should they so choose, pilgrims have the option, before embarking on their journey, to climb steps to an observation tower and view the maze. From this vantage point, the pattern is clearly visible. In contrast, viewing the maze from the ground level reveals nothing more than towering corn stalks and paths that disappear around corners. My children and I, in a prime example of collective hubris, opted to attempt the maze without looking at the pattern first. In hindsight, none of us recommend that approach.

When I began to research the life and crimes of my great-grandmother, I went forward blindly, following one lead, then another, often backtracking. It took some years to complete the journey (if it is, indeed, completed), but eventually I emerged with a pretty good sense of how things had gone. After most of the work on this book was finished, I decided to jot down some notes about our family history so that my grandchildren and their children wouldn't have to work so hard to piece things together. When I did, a few patterns emerged. Some of them were merely interesting. Others were downright spooky.

When Bertha's first husband died, she married a man ten years her junior. When my father died, my mother married a man ten years her junior (though she waited considerably longer than Bertha did to remarry). The correlation isn't significant; it's just an unusual coincidence.

Bertha had one child with her first husband, Henry Graham—a daughter, Lila, my grandmother. Lila was ten years old when her father died. (How did she feel later when her mother was suspected of having poisoned her father? We will never know; my grandmother took her feelings to the grave with her.) Lila eventually married Ernest Jefferson West, and they had one child—a daughter, Arta Ernestine, my mother. Mom was ten years old when Bertha, the mother figure in her life, was taken away forever. I was only eight years old when my father died. But my sister, the oldest daughter, was ten.

I scribbled these facts on a yellow pad at the end of a balmy summer day as I sat on my patio, a light breeze rustling the leaves of the wisteria, the pen moving faster and faster down the page as I jotted down dates, deaths and losses…and realized that my oldest daughter, my only biological daughter, was ten years old when her father and I divorced, a severance which essentially caused their estrangement for the past two decades—and counting.

Someone who believes in curses might be able to fabricate a pretty hefty one here; Bertha took her husband's life, depriving her daughter of a father, thus dooming every generation after her to experience the loss of a parent at age ten. (As I write this, my granddaughter, my daughter's oldest daughter, is ten—and a half. Both parents seem well and healthy, and as far as I know, they intend to remain married. But one never knows….)

The most significant pattern was one that, for me, constitutes a pattern of isolation. Bertha spent the last twenty-three years of her life in an institution. In the last decade before her death, she had little or no contact with family members, and she died alone, as far as we know (though I would like to believe that Gene somehow sped to her side in the waning moments of her life and was there with her as she crossed over). Her daughter, Lila, eventually moved from Detroit to Los Angeles with her second husband, Arthur Parrack. When he died, she remained in L.A., living alone in a small apartment. She never remarried and, although she would travel out to Lakewood to visit us from time to time, her contact with us diminished as she grew older. When she began to suffer from dementia, Mom moved her into assisted living, but she died shortly thereafter—alone in her room one night, twenty-four years after Arthur had died. Years ago my brother's first wife was killed in an automobile accident. The night Margaret died, my mother left her job and the roommate with whom she lived, and she went to stay with my brother, moving in with him so that she could help him care for his young children. When the time came for him to remarry, Mom moved out, and has lived alone ever since—for the past twenty-seven years. My mother will turn 90 in August of 2008.

Is this a further aspect of the curse? That each of us in turn must live the last third of her life alone?

My children have all embarked upon their adult lives, and for the first time in my life, I have begun to live alone. Am I doomed to the same fate of the grandmothers? To spend the last third of my life alone? Or will it be my sister, the oldest biological daughter? She, too, is divorced now, and though she currently lives with her two boys, the time will come when they will begin their own lives.

These are, of course, just fantastic notions, bizarre coincidences….

My mother was an innocent child of ten when her world was changed forever. She has carried the grief and shame of all that sorrow for eighty years—and counting. It is my hope that with the publication of this book, she can, at last, allow herself to be freed of those burdens, to see the truth that I have learned, to feel peace in her heart that those who have passed do not hold grudges and that her grandmother's love, as she knew it, is worth validation.

Author's Note

The related facts and incidences within these pages are true to the best of my knowledge. I have not fictionalized any part, and have tried to maintain absolute accuracy throughout; where various individuals differed in their account of events, I generally tried to assess which account had more credibility. I owe a great debt of gratitude to Marc Houseman, director of the Washington Historical Society, for fact checking the final manuscript. All that said, I know that there will be those who find what they perceive to be errors in the text. This is, after all, a history, and its landscape will be colored according to individual perspective. It is my sincere hope that readers who may disagree with specific points will still appreciate the work as a whole, for it is offered as a labor of the utmost love.